PARTY FOOD

Delicious Recipes to Get the Party Started

STERLING EPICURE
New York

STERLING EPICURE
New York

An Imprint of Sterling Publishing
387 Park Avenue South
New York, NY 10016

STERLING EPICURE is a trademark of Sterling
Publishing Co., Inc.
The distinctive Sterling logo is a registered
trademark of Sterling Publishing Co., Inc.

First published in the United Kingdom in 2013 by
Pavilion Books Company Limited

ISBN 978-1-4549-1525-6

For information about custom editions, special
sales, and premium and corporate purchases,
please contact Sterling Special Sales at 800-805-
5489 or specialsales@sterlingpublishing.com.

Manufactured in China

10 9 8 7 6 5 4 3 2 1

www.sterlingpublishing.com

NOTES

All spoon measures are level.

Ovens and broilers must be preheated to the
specified temperature.

Large eggs should be used except where otherwise
specified. Free-range eggs are recommended.

All-purpose, bread, self-rising, and wholewheat
flours should unsifted and spooned into the cup
measure and then leveled.

Note that some recipes contain raw or lightly
cooked eggs. The young, elderly, pregnant women
and anyone with an immune-deficiency disease
should avoid these because of the slight risk
of salmonella.

Contents

Dips and Breads

Mixed Italian Bruschetta

Prep time: 25 minutes

1 long, thin baguette

1 can (15-oz./425g) butter beans, drained and rinsed

a small handful of fresh mint, shredded

grated zest and juice of ½ lemon

2 tbsp. extra virgin olive oil, plus extra to drizzle

seeds from ½ pomegranate

1 cup quartered cherry tomatoes

7oz. (200g) mozzarella bocconcini, halved

1 tbsp. fresh basil pesto

2 tbsp. freshly chopped basil, plus extra leaves to garnish

a small handful of arugula

6 slices of bresaola

¼ cup freshly shaved Parmesan

½ cup sliced roasted red bell pepper

2 tbsp. black olive tapenade

salt and freshly ground black pepper

1 Cut the bread diagonally into 24 slices and toast in batches. Mash together the butter beans, mint, lemon zest and juice, and oil. Season to taste with salt and ground black pepper and stir through most of the pomegranate seeds. Set aside.

2 In a separate bowl, stir together the cherry tomatoes, mozzarella bocconcini, pesto, and basil.

3 To assemble, spoon the bean mixture onto six toasts and garnish with the remaining pomegranate seeds. Top another six with the mozzarella mixture and six with arugula, bresaola, and Parmesan. Drizzle with the oil.

4 For the final six bruschetta, put a few slices of roasted pepper on each toast. Add a little tapenade and garnish with a basil leaf.

Red Pepper and Pesto Croûtes

TAKE 5

Prep time: 20 minutes
Cooking time: about 20 minutes

1 thin baguette, cut into 24 slices
olive oil to brush
fresh pesto
4 bell pepper pieces (from a jar of marinated peppers), each sliced into 6 strips
pine nuts to garnish

1 Heat the oven to 400°F (350°F for convection ovens). Brush both sides of the bread slices with oil and put on a baking sheet. Toast in the oven for 15–20 minutes.

2 Spread 1 tsp. pesto on each croûte, then top with a pepper strip, garnish with pine nuts, and serve.

4 Fantastic Ways with Olives

Lemon and Rosemary Olives
To serve six, you will need:
a few fresh rosemary sprigs, plus
extra to garnish, 1 garlic clove,
heaped 1 cup mixed black and
green Greek olives, pared zest
of 1 lemon, 2 tbsp. vodka (optional),
1¼ cups (300ml) extra virgin
olive oil.

1   Put the rosemary and garlic in a
small heatproof bowl and pour
enough boiling water to cover
over. Leave for 1–2 minutes, then
drain well.
2   Put the olives, lemon zest, and
vodka, if using, in a glass jar and
add the rosemary and garlic.
Pour over enough oil to cover the
olives. Cover and chill for at least
24 hours before using.
3   To serve, remove the olives from
the oil and garnish with sprigs
of fresh rosemary. Use within
one week.

SAVE MONEY

Don't waste the flavored oil
that's left over from the olives.
It's perfect for using in salad
dressings and marinades.

Tapenade

To serve four, you will need:
3 tbsp. rinsed and drained capers,
½ cup pitted black olives, 1 drained
can (2-oz./50g) anchovy fillets in
oil, 7 tbsp. olive oil, 2 tbsp. brandy,
freshly ground black pepper, and
vegetable sticks, grilled vegetables,
or toasted baguette to serve.

1   Put the capers into a blender or
    food processor with the olives
    and anchovies. Process briefly
    to chop.
2   With the motor running, add
    the oil in a steady stream. Stir
    in the brandy and season with
    pepper to taste. Transfer to a
    serving bowl.
3   Serve the tapenade with
    raw vegetable sticks, grilled
    vegetables, or toasted baguette
    slices.

Black Olive Hummus

To serve six, you will need:
1 drained and rinsed can
(15-oz./425g) chickpeas, juice of
1 lemon, 4 tbsp. tahini, 1 tsp.
paprika, 1 crushed garlic clove,
5 tbsp. extra virgin olive oil, salt
and freshly ground black pepper,
¼ cup roughly chopped pitted
black olives, and warm pita
bread (see page 20) or toasted
flatbreads to serve.

1 Put the chickpeas, lemon juice,
   tahini, paprika, garlic, and oil
   in a blender or food processor.
   Season generously with salt and
   ground black pepper, then blend
   to a paste. Stir in the chopped
   black olives.
2 Spoon the hummus into a
   serving bowl, then cover and
   chill until needed.
3 Sprinkle with a little extra
   paprika and extra virgin olive
   oil, if you like, and serve with
   warm pita bread or toasted
   flatbreads.

Black Olive Bread

To make two loaves, you will need:
2 tsp. active dry yeast, 4 cups white
bread flour, plus extra to dust,
2 tsp. coarse sea salt, plus extra to
sprinkle, 6 tbsp. extra virgin olive
oil, plus extra to grease, ⅔ cup
pitted and chopped black olives.

1 Put ⅔ cup (150ml) hand-hot
   water into a bowl, stir in the
   yeast, and leave for 10 minutes,
   or until frothy. Put the flour into
   a bowl or a food processor, then
   add the salt, yeast mix, ¾ cup
   plus 2 tbsp. warm water, and
   2 tbsp. oil. Using a wooden
   spoon or the dough hook, mix
   for 2–3 minutes to make a soft,
   smooth dough. Put the dough
   into a lightly greased bowl, cover
   with greased plastic wrap, and
   leave it in a warm place for 45
   minutes, or until doubled in size.

2 Punch down the dough to knock
   out the air, then knead on a
   lightly floured work surface for
   1 minute. Add the olives and
   knead until combined. Divide in
   half, shape into rectangles, and
   put into two greased pans, each
   about 10 × 6in. (25 × 15cm). Cover
   with plastic wrap and leave in
   a warm place for 1 hour, or until
   the dough is puffy.

3 Heat the oven to 400°F (350°F for
   convection ovens). Press
   your finger into the dough
   12 times, drizzle 2 tbsp. oil over
   the surface, and sprinkle with
   salt. Bake for 30–35 minutes
   until golden. Drizzle with the
   remaining oil. Slice and serve
   while warm.

Classic Hummus

Prep time: 10 minutes

1 can (15-oz./425g) chickpeas
3 tbsp. olive oil, plus extra to drizzle
1½ tsp. lemon juice
1 small garlic clove
¼ tsp. ground cumin
sprinkle of paprika or cayenne pepper
   (optional)
salt and freshly ground black pepper
toasted pita bread (see page 20) and
   breadsticks to serve

1 Drain and rinse the chickpeas. Put a spoonful to one side and put the rest into a food processor with the oil, lemon juice, 1 tbsp. water, garlic clove, ground cumin, and seasoning.

2 Blend until smooth, then check the seasoning. Scrape into a serving dish. Garnish with the reserved chickpeas, a sprinkle of paprika or cayenne pepper (if you have it), and a drizzle of olive oil. Serve with toasted pita bread and breadsticks for scooping.

Serves 6

Naan

Prep time: 20 minutes, plus rising
Cooking time: about 12 minutes

½oz. (15g) fresh yeast or 1½ tsp. active
   dry yeast
about ⅔ cup (150ml) lukewarm milk
3⅔ cups all-purpose flour, plus extra
   to dust
1 tsp. baking powder
½ tsp. salt
2 tsp. sugar
1 egg, beaten
2 tbsp. vegetable oil, plus extra
   to grease
4 tbsp. plain yogurt

1 Blend the fresh yeast with the milk.
   If using dry yeast, sprinkle it into
   the milk and leave in a warm place
   for 15 minutes, or until frothy.
2 Sift the flour, baking powder, and
   salt into a large bowl. Make a well
   in the middle and stir in the sugar,
   egg, oil, and yogurt. Add the yeast
   liquid and mix well to a soft dough,
   adding more milk if necessary.
   Turn the dough out onto a lightly
floured work surface and knead
well for 10 minutes, or until smooth
and elastic.

3 Place the dough in a bowl, cover
   with greased plastic wrap, and let
   rise in a warm place for about 1 hour
   until doubled in size.
4 Heat the broiler. Knead the dough
   on a lightly floured work surface for
   2–3 minutes, then divide into six
   equal pieces. Roll out each piece on
   a lightly floured work surface and
   shape into a large teardrop about
   10in. (25cm) long.
5 Place a piece of the naan dough on
   a cookie sheet and put under the
   broiler. Cook for 1½–2 minutes on
   each side until golden brown and
   puffy. Cook the remaining naan in
   the same way. Serve warm.

Makes 6

Pita Bread

Prep time 20 minutes, plus rising
Cooking time: about 8 minutes per batch, plus cooling

½oz. (15g) fresh yeast or 1½ tsp. active
dry yeast and 1 tsp. sugar

5⅔ cups white bread flour, plus extra
to dust

1 tsp. salt

1 tbsp. sugar

1 tbsp. olive oil, plus extra to grease

1 Blend the fresh yeast with scant
2 cups (450ml) lukewarm water. If
using dried yeast, sprinkle it into the
water with the sugar and leave in a
warm place for 15 minutes, or until
frothy.

2 Put the flour, salt, and sugar into
a bowl, make a well in the middle,
and pour in the yeast liquid with
the oil. Mix to a smooth dough, then
turn out onto a lightly floured work
surface and knead for 10 minutes, or
until smooth and elastic.

3 Place the dough in a large bowl, cover
with greased plastic wrap, and let rise
in a warm place until doubled in size.

4 Divide the dough into 16 pieces and
roll each into an oval shape about 8in.
(20cm) long. Place on floured cookie
sheets, cover with greased plastic
wrap, and leave in a warm place for
about 30 minutes until slightly risen
and puffy. Heat the oven to 475°F
(425°F for convection ovens).

5 Bake the pitas in batches for
5–8 minutes only. They should
be just lightly browned on top.
Remove from the oven and wrap
in a clean dish towel. Repeat with
the remaining pitas.

6 When the pitas are warm enough
to handle, but not completely cold,
transfer them to a plastic bag and
leave until cold. This guarantees
they have a soft crust.

7 To serve, warm in the oven, or toast
lightly. Split and fill with salad
ingredients, cheese, cold meats, or
your favorite sandwich filling. Or,
cut into strips and serve with dips.

Makes 16

Tzatziki

To serve eight, you will need:
1 cucumber, 1¼ cups Greek-style yogurt, 2 tsp. olive oil, 2 tbsp. freshly chopped mint, 1 large crushed garlic clove, salt and freshly ground black pepper, and warm pita bread (see page 20), and vegetable sticks to serve.

1 Halve, seed, and dice the cucumber and put into a bowl.
2 Add the yogurt and olive oil. Stir in the chopped mint and garlic, and season with salt and ground black pepper to taste. Cover and chill in the refrigerator until ready to serve.
3 Serve with warm pita bread and vegetable sticks.

Taramasalata

To serve six, you will need:
3½oz. (100g) country-style bread with the crusts removed (about 3 slices), 3oz. (75g) smoked cod roe, 2 tbsp. lemon juice, 7 tbsp. light olive oil, ground black pepper, and warm pita bread (see page 20) or toasted flatbreads to serve.

1 Put the bread into a bowl, cover with cold water, and let soak for 10 minutes. Drain and squeeze out most of the water.
2 Soak the smoked cod roe in cold water to cover for 10 minutes, then drain and remove the skin.
3 Put the roe in a blender or food processor with the bread and blend for 30 seconds. With the motor running, add the lemon juice and oil, then blend briefly to combine. Season with ground black pepper to taste.
4 Spoon into a bowl, cover, and chill until needed. Serve with warm pita bread or toasted flatbreads.

Blue Cheese Dip

To serve six, you will need:
⅔ cup (150ml) sour cream,
1 crushed garlic clove, 6oz. (175g)
blue cheese, juice of 1 lemon,
salt and freshly ground black
pepper, snipped chives to garnish,
vegetable sticks to serve.

1 Put all the ingredients into a
   blender or food processor and
   work to a smooth paste.
2 Transfer to a serving dish and
   chill until required. Check the
   seasoning, sprinkle with chives,
   and serve with a selection of
   vegetable sticks.

Guacamole

To serve six, you will need:
2 ripe avocados, 2 seeded and
chopped small tomatoes, juice of
2 limes, 2 tbsp. extra virgin olive oil,
2 tbsp. freshly chopped cilantro, salt
and freshly ground black pepper,
and tortilla chips or warm pita
bread (see page 20), and vegetable
sticks to serve.

1 Cut the avocados in half, remove
   the pits, and peel away the skin.
   Tip the flesh into a bowl and
   mash with a fork.
2 Quickly add the tomatoes, lime
   juice, oil, and chopped cilantro.
   Mix well and season with salt
   and ground black pepper to
   taste. Cover and chill until ready
   to serve.
3 Serve the guacamole with
   tortilla chips or warm pita bread
   and vegetable sticks.

Red Pepper and Feta Dip

To make about ¾ cup, you will
need: 1 drained jar (11-oz./300g)
roasted red peppers, 1½ cups
crumbled feta, 1 small garlic clove,
1 tbsp. plain yogurt, and toasted
pita bread (see page 20) to serve.

1 Put all the ingredients into a
   blender or food processor and
   blend until smooth. Serve the
   dip with strips of toasted
   pita bread.

Tortilla Chips for Dips

TAKE 5

🍴 **Prep time:** 10 minutes
🍴 **Cooking time:** about 20 minutes, plus cooling

8 flour tortillas
2 tbsp. olive oil
¼–½ tsp. smoked paprika
salt
dips to serve

SAVE TIME

Make up to two days ahead.
Keep in an airtight container.

1 Heat the oven to 400°F (350°F for convection ovens). Stack the flour tortillas on top of each other, then cut through the stack like a pizza to make eight wedges. Put the triangles into a large bowl with the oil, smoked paprika, and lots of salt.

2 Use your hands to mix everything together, making sure all the triangles are covered with oil and spice. Divide the triangles between two cookie sheets.

3 Toast for 12–20 minutes, tossing occasionally, until golden and crisp. Let cool completely before serving with your favorite dips.

Serves 10

Take 5 Quick & Easy Salsas

Quick Tomato

Put 4 roughly chopped tomatoes, ½ ripe, peeled and roughly chopped avocado, 1 tsp. olive oil, and the juice of ½ lime in a bowl and stir well. Use for broiled and grilled fish or chicken.

Smoky

Put ½ cup finely chopped onions or shallots, ⅔ cup (150ml) bottled barbecue sauce, 7 tbsp. maple syrup, 1 tbsp. apple cider vinegar, 1 tbsp. soft brown sugar, 7 tbsp. water, 1 tsp. lemon juice, and a little grated lemon zest in a pan. Bring to a boil and let boil for 10–15 minutes until syrupy. Take the pan off the heat and add 6 finely chopped scallions, and ¾ cup finely chopped fresh pineapple. Serve warm or cold. Use for burgers.

Mango and Fennel

Put 1 halved and diced mango, 1 small trimmed and diced fennel bulb, 1 seeded and finely diced chili pepper (See Safety Tip, page 38), 1 tbsp. balsamic vinegar, 2 tbsp. freshly chopped flat-leaf parsley, and 2 tbsp. freshly chopped mint into a bowl. Add the juice of 1 lime, stir to combine, and season generously with salt and ground black pepper. Use for broiled and grilled chicken.

Avocado, Tomato, and Cilantro

Put 1 chopped red onion in a bowl with 1 ripe, peeled and chopped avocado, 4 large roughly chopped tomatoes, a small handful of roughly chopped fresh cilantro, and the juice of 1 lime. Mix well, then season with salt and ground black pepper. Use at once for boiled or grilled pork chops or chicken.

Shrimp and Avocado

Put 2 large ripe, peeled and roughly chopped avocados in a large bowl, then add 12oz. (350g) shelled, cooked jumbo shrimp, 6 thinly sliced small scallions, 3 tbsp. freshly chopped cilantro, the grated zest and juice of 3 limes, and ½ cup olive oil. Mix well, then season with salt and ground black pepper. Use for smoked salmon or broiled or grilled fish.

Parmesan and Olive Grissini

🍴 **Prep time:** 20 minutes, plus kneading and rising
Cooking time: about 20 minutes, plus cooling

1 tsp. instant dry yeast

4 cups white bread flour, plus extra
   to dust

1 tsp. salt

3 tbsp. olive oil

2 tsp. sugar

⅓ cup finely chopped pitted
   black olives

½ cup freshly grated Parmesan

To finish

oil to grease

semolina to dust

beaten egg to glaze

coarse salt flakes to sprinkle

1 Put all the dough ingredients, except the olives and Parmesan, into the bread-maker bucket with 1¼ cups (300ml) water, following the order and method specified in the manual.

2 Fit the bucket into the bread maker and set to the dough program with rising setting, if applicable. Press start. Add the olives and Parmesan when the machine beeps, or halfway through the kneading cycle. Lightly oil two large cookie sheets and sprinkle with semolina.

3 Once the dough is ready, turn out onto a work surface and punch it down to deflate. Cover with a dish towel and let rest for 10 minutes.

4 Lightly flour the work surface and roll out the dough to a 12 × 8 in. (30 × 20cm) rectangle, cover loosely with a dish towel, and leave for 30 minutes until well risen.

5 Heat the oven to 425°F (400°F for convection ovens). Cut the dough

TRY THIS

For convenience, make these several days in advance and store in an airtight container. To serve, pop them into a medium oven for a couple of minutes if they have softened slightly.

Makes 32

across the width into four thick bands. From each of these, cut eight very thin strips and transfer them to the baking sheet, stretching each one until it is about 11in. (27.5cm) long, and spacing the strips ½in. (1cm) apart.

6 Brush very lightly with beaten egg and sprinkle with salt flakes. Bake for 18–20 minutes until crisp and golden. Transfer the grissini to a wire rack to cool.

Cheese Straws

Prep time: 10 minutes, plus chilling
Cooking time: about 20 minutes, plus cooling

1⅔ cups self-rising flour, sifted, plus
   extra to dust
a pinch of cayenne pepper
1 stick unsalted butter, diced and
   chilled, plus extra to grease
1¼ cups freshly grated Parmesan
2 eggs
1 tsp. English mustard
sesame and poppy seeds to sprinkle

1 Put the flour, cayenne, and butter
  into a food processor and pulse
  until the mixture resembles bread
  crumbs. (Alternatively, cut the
  butter into the flour and cayenne
  in a large bowl by hand, until it
  resembles fine crumbs.) Add the
  Parmesan and mix in.

2 Crack one egg into a bowl. Separate
  the other egg, then put the white to
  one side and add the egg yolk to the
  bowl with the whole egg. Mix in the
  mustard. Add to the flour mixture
and mix together. Lightly flour
a cutting board, tip the mixture onto
the board and knead lightly for
30 seconds, then wrap in plastic
wrap and chill in the refrigerator for
30 minutes.

3 Heat the oven to 350°F (300°F for
  convection ovens). Grease two
  cookie sheets. Roll out the dough on
  a lightly floured work surface to a
  12 × 9in. (30 x 22.5cm) rectangle. Cut
  out 24 equal straws and carefully
  twist each straw twice. Put on the
  cookie sheets.

4 Beat the reserved egg white with
  a fork until frothy and brush over
  the cheese straws, then sprinkle
  with the sesame and poppy seeds.
  Bake for 18–20 minutes until golden.
  Remove from the oven and cool for
  5 minutes, then transfer to a wire
  rack and cool completely.

Makes 24

Herb Vinegar

To make 2½ cups (600ml), you will need: 1oz. (25g) fresh herbs, 2½ cups (600ml) red or white wine vinegar.

1 Put the herbs and vinegar into a pan and bring to a boil. Pour into a heatproof bowl, cover, and let soak overnight.
2 Strain through a cheesecloth-lined sieve and bottle. Store for one week before using.

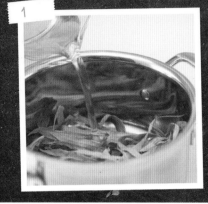

Garlic, Soy, and Honey

To make about 7 tbsp. you will need: 1 crushed garlic clove, 2 tsp. each soy sauce and honey, 1 tbsp. apple cider vinegar, 4 tbsp. olive oil, ground black pepper.

1 Put the garlic in a small bowl. Add the soy sauce, honey, vinegar, and oil, season to taste with pepper and whisk together thoroughly.
2 If not using, store in a cool place and whisk briefly before using.

Lemon Vinaigrette

To make about ⅔ cup (150ml), you will need: 2 tbsp. lemon juice, 2 tsp. honey, ½ cup extra virgin olive oil, 3 tbsp. freshly chopped mint, 4 tbsp. roughly chopped flat-leaf parsley, salt and freshly ground black pepper.

1 Put the lemon juice, honey, and seasoning to taste in a bowl and whisk to combine. Gradually whisk in the oil and stir in the herbs.
2 If not using immediately, store in a cool place and whisk before using.

Sun-Dried Tomato

To make about 7 tbsp., you will need: 2 drained sun-dried tomatoes in oil, 2 tbsp. oil from sun-dried tomato jar, 2 tbsp. red wine vinegar, 1 garlic clove, 1 tbsp. sun-dried tomato paste, a pinch of sugar (optional), 2 tbsp. extra virgin olive oil, salt and freshly ground black pepper.

1   Put the sun-dried tomatoes and oil, the vinegar, garlic, and tomato paste into a blender or food processor. Add the sugar, if you like.
2   With the motor running, pour the oil through the feeder tube and blend briefly to make a fairly thick dressing. Season to taste with salt and ground black pepper.
3   If not using store in a cool place and whisk briefly before using.

Fruit Vinegar

To make 2½ cups (600ml), you will need: 1lb. (450g) raspberries and blackberries, 2½ cups (600ml) red wine vinegar.

1   Put the fruit into a nonmetallic bowl and, using the back of a spoon, break it up, then add the vinegar. Cover and let stand for three days, stirring now and then.
2   Strain through a cheesecloth-lined sieve and bottle. Store for two weeks before using.

Dazzling Canapés

Easy Ways To Plan Your Party

Use this handy guide to help you plan the perfect event.

Entertaining

Plan ahead and you are more likely to enjoy the occasion. Avoid planning a meal that is too complicated, and don't tackle a recipe that is totally unfamiliar— have a practice run first. When deciding on a menu, keep it as well balanced as possible. Think about the colors, flavors, and textures of the foods—rich and light, sweet and savory, crunchy and smooth, hot and cold. Don't have cream or fruit featuring in all the courses; avoid an all-brown menu.

Select produce in season, for the best flavor and value for money. Check whether any of your guests have special dietary needs and plan appropriately. Try to cook an entirely meatless meal even if there is going to be just one vegetarian— it's not as difficult as it sounds, and rarely does anybody notice!

It is worthwhile choosing dishes that can be prepared well ahead of time or prepared up to a certain point, only needing a little last-minute finishing in the kitchen.

Planning the event

Make a master shopping list and separate lists of dishes to be prepared ahead, with a note of when to make them. Plan refrigerator and freezer space; for a large party, you might need to make different arrangements, such as asking your neighbor to keep some foods in their refrigerator, or putting bulky items into cool boxes. Check that you have candles if you are using.

Make invitations to a dinner party over the phone ten to twelve days in advance. Mention whether it's a formal or informal occasion, the date and time, address if necessary, and say if there are any special dress requirements to avoid embarrassing situations! If you are sending written invitations, mail them two to three weeks in advance.

Check that table linen is laundered and ironed ahead of time, and that glasses and silverware are clean and polished. Clean the house a day or two ahead. Buy or order wine and drinks in advance, and avoid doing all the shopping at once.

Handy hints for entertaining

Try to strike a good balance between hot and cold items, as well as light and substantial dishes. Most supermarkets have a good selection of ready-to-eat or -cook appetizers, if you don't have time to make them. You can also use good-quality bought ingredients, such as mayonnaise and fresh sauces, to save time.

- A freezer is invaluable when entertaining, whether on a grand scale or just dinner for two.
- Keep a supply of ready-to-bake bread in the refrigerator or freezer for quick fresh bread. Freeze packages of half-baked breads to pop in the oven as and when needed.
- Keep a supply of premium ice cream in the freezer.
- Remember to unwrap cheeses and bring them to room temperature at least one hour before serving, keeping them lightly covered, to prevent them drying out, until the last minute.
- Make ice well in advance.
- During the winter, if you run out of refrigerator space, use a greenhouse or garage to keep drinks and perishables cold.
- Use the microwave to reheat cooked vegetables, sauces, and gravy.
- Decide in advance where you are going to stack dirty plates. A kitchen overflowing with dirty dishes looks unsightly, so consider paying someone to do this for you on the day.

Spicy Nuts

Prep time: 10 minutes
Cooking time: about 20 minutes, plus cooling

4 cups mixed unsalted nuts and seeds, such as hazelnuts, peanuts, cashews, macadamias, Brazil nuts, pumpkin, and sunflower seeds

2 tbsp. olive oil

1–2 red chili peppers, seeded and finely chopped (see Safety Tip)

1½ tbsp. fresh thyme leaves

2 garlic cloves, finely chopped

1¼ tsp. coarse sea salt

freshly ground black pepper

1 Heat the oven to 400°F (350°F for convection ovens). Mix together all the ingredients in a large bowl with the sea salt and lots of pepper.

2 Put the nut mixture on a baking sheet and roast for 15–20 minutes, tossing occasionally, until the nuts are golden. Let cool completely, then empty into bowls and serve.

TRY THIS

Complete the recipe up to a week in advance. Cool, then transfer to an airtight container and store at room temperature.

SAFETY TIP

Chili peppers can be very mild to blisteringly hot, depending on the type of chili pepper and its ripeness. Taste a small piece first to check it's not too hot for you. Be extremely careful when handling chili peppers and not to touch or rub your eyes with your fingers, or they will sting. Wash knives immediately after cutting chili peppers. As a precaution, use rubber gloves when preparing them, if you like.

Makes 4 cups

Popadum Scoops

🍴 **Prep time:** 10 minutes

¼ red onion, finely chopped

1 ripe mango, peeled, pitted, and finely diced

½ green chili pepper, seeded and finely chopped (see Safety Tip, page 38)

a small handful of fresh cilantro, finely chopped

grated zest and juice of 1 lime

20 mini popadums

salt and freshly ground black pepper

SAVE TIME

Complete the recipe up the end of step 1 one day in advance, but don't add the cilantro. Cover and chill in the refrigerator, then complete the recipe up to 1 hour before serving.

1 Mix the onion, mango, chili pepper, cilantro, lime zest and juice, and some seasoning together in a nonmetallic bowl.

2 Spoon into papadums and serve.

Mini Eggs Benedict

Prep time: 20 minutes
Cooking time: about 5 minutes

vegetable oil to grease

12 quail eggs

3 standard, thin white bread slices

1 tbsp. mayonnaise or bought
  hollandaise sauce

2–3 ham slices

freshly ground black pepper

1 Bring a medium pot one-quarter filled with water to a simmer. Grease a baking sheet, then put the baking sheet on top of the pan to heat. Carefully crack all the quail eggs into a bowl, then gently pour the eggs onto the hot tray, moving the yolks so they are not touching one another. The steam will cook the eggs in 3–5 minutes.

2 Meanwhile, toast the bread slices. Use a 1½in. (4cm) round cookie cutter to stamp out 12 circles of toast. Top each circle with a dab of mayonnaise or hollandaise. Next, stamp out ham circles with the same cutter and put one circle on each toast stack.

3 When the egg whites are cooked (and the yolks are still soft), lift the tray off the steam. Use the cutter to stamp around each yolk and use a metal spatula to transfer the egg circles to the stacks. Grind some black pepper over and serve.

SAVE TIME

These mini eggs are best made fresh, but will sit happily for up to 30 minutes once assembled.

Makes 12

Scotch Quail Eggs

Prep time: 25 minutes
Cooking time: about 20 minutes

all-purpose flour to dust

1 extra-large egg, lightly beaten

¾ cup dried bread crumbs

12 hard-boiled quail eggs

11oz. (300g) pork sausage meat

2–3 tbsp. vegetable oil to fry

sea salt and mustard to serve

1 Heat the oven to 400°F (350°F for convection ovens). Put some flour, the egg, and bread crumbs into separate small bowls.

2 Divide the sausage meat into 12 equal portions. With lightly floured hands, form a portion into a flat patty about 2½in. (6.25cm) across in the palm of one hand. Put a greased quail egg in the middle, then shape the sausage meat around it. Set aside on a board and repeat with the remaining eggs and sausage meat.

3 Dip the covered eggs in the flour and tap off excess, then dip in the beaten egg and coat in the bread crumbs.

4 Heat the oil in a large skillet over medium-high heat. Add the coated eggs and fry, turning regularly, until golden on each side. (Fry in batches if necessary.) Transfer to a baking sheet.

5 Cook the eggs in the oven for 10 minutes. Serve warm or at room temperature (sliced in half, if you like) with sea salt and mustard.

TRY THIS

Hard-boil quail eggs up to two days ahead. Cool, shell, cover, and chill. Complete the recipe up to a day ahead, if you want. Cool and chill. Let come up to room temperature, or warm in a 350°F oven (300°F for convection ovens) for 5–10 minutes before serving.

Makes 12

Mini Baked Potatoes

Prep time: 20 minutes
Cooking time: about 40 minutes

20 baby new potatoes
1 tbsp. vegetable oil
7 tbsp. crème fraîche or sour cream
finely grated zest and juice of 1 lemon
1 tbsp. freshly chopped dill, plus extra
   to garnish
3½oz. (100g) smoked salmon strips
lumpfish caviar
salt and freshly ground black pepper

1. Heat the oven to 400°F (350°F for convection ovens). Put the potatoes in a roasting pan and toss through the oil and plenty of seasoning. Roast for 35–40 minutes until golden and tender. Let cool to room temperature.

2. In a small bowl, stir together the crème fraîche, lemon zest and juice, dill, and seasoning.

3. Cut a slit down the length of a potato, then squeeze the sides apart a little to open. Repeat with remaining potatoes. Top each with a dollop of the crème fraîche mixture, a curl of salmon, a few caviar eggs, and a dill frond. Serve.

Makes 20

Loaded Potato Skins

Prep time: 15 minutes
Cooking time: about 1½ hours, plus cooling

4 Idaho potatoes
½ tbsp. wholegrain mustard
1 tbsp. freshly snipped chives
¾ cup grated cheddar cheese
4 tbsp. sour cream
2 egg yolks
1 tbsp. olive oil
salt and freshly ground black pepper
ketchup and barbecue sauce to serve
   (optional)

1 Heat the oven to 400°F (350°F for convection ovens). Prick each potato a few times with a fork and roast for 1–1¼ hours until the potato can be easily pierced with a knife. Leave until cool enough to handle.

2 Carefully halve each potato, then cut each half into three long wedges. Scoop most of the flesh into a bowl, leaving just enough attached to the skin to maintain its shape. Arrange the wedges skin-side down on a large baking sheet.

3 To the potato flesh, add the mustard, snipped chives, grated cheese, sour cream, egg yolks, oil, and plenty of seasoning.

4 Load the filling onto the skins and bake in the oven for 15–20 minutes until golden. Leave the wedges to cool for at least 10 minutes before serving on their own, or with ketchup or barbecue sauce.

TRY THIS

Prepare and fill the potato skins up to 4 hours ahead. Cover and chill. To serve, uncover and complete the recipe.

Makes 24

Thai Crab Cups

🍴 **Prep time:** 15 minutes

3½oz. (100g) white crabmeat

1½ tsp. Thai fish sauce

2½ tbsp. mayonnaise

½–1 red chili pepper, seeded and finely
chopped (see Safety Tip, page 38)

a small handful of fresh cilantro,
chopped, plus extra to garnish
(optional)

15 mini croustade cases, thawed
if frozen

salt and freshly ground black pepper

SAVE TIME

Make the crab mixture up
to a day ahead, but don't add
the cilantro. Cover and chill.
Complete the recipe to serve.

1 In a medium bowl, stir together
the first five ingredients. Check the
seasoning and adjust to taste. Fill
each croustade case with a spoonful
of the crab mixture, then garnish
with extra cilantro, if you like.

Makes 15

Party Shrimp

Prep time: 10 minutes
Cooking time: about 5 minutes

5–7 slices of bacon

5oz. (150g) shelled jumbo shrimp

2 tbsp. butter

1 tbsp. snipped fresh chives

freshly ground black pepper

1 Cut each bacon slice in half lengthwise, then in half widthwise. Wrap a bacon strip around the middle of each raw shrimp.

2 Melt the butter in a large skillet. Add the shrimp and cook for 3–5 minutes until the shrimp are bright pink and bacon is cooked.

3 Season well with ground black pepper and sprinkle the chives over. Serve immediately with cocktail picks.

TRY THIS

Complete the recipe to the end of step 1 up to 4 hours in advance. Cover and keep in the refrigerator, then complete the recipe to serve.

Makes about 25

Smoked Fish Bites

Prep time: 15 minutes

7 tbsp. cream cheese
3½oz. (100g) skinned smoked fish, such as mackerel
finely grated zest of 1 lemon
3 slices or rye bread, about 5oz. (150g)
1 tbsp. fresh snipped chives
salt and freshly ground black pepper

SAVE TIME

Assemble these canapés up to 4 hours ahead, cover, and keep in the refrigerator. Alternatively, prepare to the end of step 1 up to two days ahead. Cover and chill the mixture. Complete the recipe to serve.

1 Put the cream cheese into a food processor. Add the skinned smoked fish, lemon zest, and some seasoning. Pulse briefly until well combined, but still with some texture. Empty into a bowl.

2 Cut each slice of rye bread into nine equal pieces. Use a knife to smear some fish pâté onto each piece of bread. Garnish with freshly cracked black pepper and chives.

Makes 27

Sweet Onion Sausage Rolls

Prep time: 20 minutes, plus chilling
Cooking time: about 15 minutes

11oz. (300g) sausage meat
a small handful of fresh parsley,
  finely chopped
13oz. (375g) bought piecrust dough in
  a rectangular sheet, thawed if frozen
2 tbsp. onion relish
1 extra-large egg, lightly beaten
poppy seeds to sprinkle

1 Put the sausage meat into a large
  bowl and stir in the parsley.
  Unroll the piecrust dough and cut
  lengthwise into four equal strips.
  Thinly spread 1 tbsp. of the onion
  marmalade lengthwise down the
  middle of one of the strips. Repeat
  with one other strip.

2 Divide the sausage mixture in half.
  Shape one half into a thin cylinder
  as long as the pastry strips, then
  position it on top of one of the
  relish-covered strips. Repeat with
  the remaining sausage mixture.
  Brush the visible dough around the
  sausage cylinders with beaten egg,
  then top with the remaining dough
  strips. Press down on the edges
  to seal. Transfer to a cookie sheet
  and chill for 30 minutes.

3 Heat the oven to 400°F (350°F for
  convection ovens). Line two cookie
  sheets with parchment paper. Brush
  both rolls with egg and sprinkle
  over some poppy seeds. Cut into
  1½in. (4cm) pieces and place on the
  prepared cookie sheets. Cook for
  15 minutes, or until golden. Serve
  warm or at room temperature.

SAVE TIME

Complete up to end of step 2 up
to one day ahead. Cover and chill.
Complete the recipe to serve.

Makes about 22

Mini Hotdogs

Prep time: 25 minutes, plus chilling
Cooking time: about 40 minutes

1 tbsp. vegetable oil

1 onion, thinly sliced

13oz. (375g) piecrust dough in a
    rectangular sheet, thawed if frozen

all-purpose flour, to dust

24 raw mini hotdogs

1 egg, lightly beaten

mustard and ketchup to serve

1 Heat the oil in a skillet and slowly cook the onion for 10 minutes, or until softened but not colored.

2 Unroll the dough onto a lightly floured work surface and trim the edges to neaten. Cut out 24 squares, each measuring 2½in. (6.25cm). Put a pinch of onion in a line down the middle of each square and top with a hotdog, laid straight or diagonally across the dough. Lift the empty dough up and stick to the sides of the hotdog. Transfer to a baking sheet. Complete with the remaining pastry, onion, and hotdogs. Brush the hotdogs all over with beaten egg and chill for 10 minutes.

3 Heat the oven to 400°F (350°F for convection ovens). Cook the hotdogs in the oven for 25–30 minutes until golden. Cool for 5 minutes. Serve warm or at room temperature with a squeeze of mustard or ketchup.

SAVE TIME

Make the hot dogs to the end of step 2 up to one day ahead. Loosely cover and chill. To serve, brush with more beaten egg and complete the recipe.

Makes 24

Harissa Chicken Balls with Yogurt Dip

Prep time: 20 minutes
Cooking time: about 25 minutes

2 boneless, skinless chicken breast
   halves

1½–2 tsp. rose harissa paste, to taste

finely grated zest of ½ orange

2 scallions

2 tbsp. olive oil

salt and freshly ground black pepper

For the dip

½ cup plain yogurt

few fresh mint leaves, thinly sliced

2in. (5cm) cucumber, grated

SAVE TIME

Cook the chicken balls up to
a day ahead. Cool, cover, and
chill. Make dip up to 3 hours
ahead. Chill. To serve, reheat the
chicken balls in an oven heated
to 325°F (275°F for convection
ovens) for 10 minutes. Stir the
dip before serving.

1 Put the chicken, harissa, orange
zest, and some seasoning into a food
processor. Snip in the scallions, then
blend until fairly smooth. Remove
the blade and shape the mixture
into bite-size balls.

2 Heat the oil over a medium heat
in a large, nonstick skillet. Add
the chicken balls (you will need
to do this in batches) and fry for
10–12 minutes, turning frequently,
until golden and cooked through;
check by cutting into one. Set aside.

3 To make the dip, mix all the
ingredients together with some
seasoning and put into a small
serving bowl. Serve the chicken
balls warm or at room temperature
with the dip on the side.

Makes about 28

Tangerine Shots

Prep time: 10 minutes, plus chilling
Cooking time: about 3 minutes

5 gelatin leaves
12 tangerines, about 2¼lb. (1kg)
¾ cup sugar
whipped cream, to serve (optional)

1 Put the gelatin in a bowl and cover
with cold water. Let soak for
5 minutes. Meanwhile, zest
2 tangerines and put the zest into
a large pan. Squeeze the juice from
the zested and whole tangerines
and add to the pan with the sugar.

2 Lift the gelatin out of the water
(discard the water) and add to the
pan. Heat slowly until the sugar
dissolves. Strain the mixture into
a large pitcher with a good pouring
spout and make up to 4¼ cups (1 liter)
with cold water. Pour the mixture
into 12 small glasses and chill in
the refrigerator for at least 5 hours,
preferably overnight.

3 To serve, take the gelled shots out
of refrigerator 5 minutes before you
need them to let soften slightly.
Serve with spoons and topped with
whipped cream, if you like.

TRY THIS

Make these delicious gelled shots
up to two days ahead.

62

Makes 12

Perfect Catering

The tables below show approximate quantities to serve 12 people.
For 25, multiply the quantities by 2; and for 50, multiply by 4.
When dealing with larger numbers, say for 75, multiply by 5½, and
for 100, multiply by 7.

First courses

Soups	2½ quarts (2.6 liters)
Pâtés	2½lb. (1.1kg)
Smoked salmon	2lb. (900g)
Shrimp	2lb. (900g)

Main dishes

Boneless chicken or turkey	4lb. (1.8kg)
Whole chicken	three 3lb. (1.4kg) oven-ready birds
Turkey	one 12lb. (5.4kg) oven-ready bird

Lamb/beef/pork

Boneless	4½–5lb. (2–2.3kg)
On the bone	7–8lb. (3.2–3.6kg)
Chopped	4½lb. (2kg)

Fish

Whole with head	5lb. (2.3kg)
Steaks	twelve 6oz. (175g) steaks
Fillets	4½lb. (2kg)
Shrimp (main course)	3lb. (1.4kg)

Turkey

6–10 people	5–8lb. (2.3–3.6kg)
10–15	8–11lb. (3.6–5kg)
15–20	11–15lb (5–6.8kg)

Accompaniments

Roast and mashed potatoes	4½lb. (2kg)
New potatoes	4lb. (1.8kg)
Rice and pasta	1½lb. (700g)
Green vegetables	3lb. (1.4kg)
Fresh spinach	8lb. (3.6kg)

Salads

Tomatoes	1½lb. (700g)
Salad leaves	2 medium heads
Cucumber	1 large
French dressing	¾–1 cup

Bread

Fresh uncut bread	1 large loaf
Medium sliced loaf	1 large (approximately 24 slices)

Cheese

For a cheese and wine party	3lb. (1.4kg)
To serve at the end of a meal	1½lb. (700g)

Butter

To serve with bread or crackers and cheese	2 sticks
To serve with bread and crackers and cheese	12oz. (350g)
For sandwiches	1½ sticks softened butter for 12 rounds

Cream

For desserts	2½ cups (600ml) heavy cream
For coffee	1¼ cups (300ml)

Coffee and tea

Ground coffee	4oz. (125g) for 12 medium cups
Instant	3oz. (75g) for 12 large cups
Milk	allow 2 cups (450ml) for 12 cups of tea

Afternoon Tea Party

Perfect Sandwiches and Dips

Party sandwiches don't have to be dull. All you need is a little imagination and lots of delicious fillings.

Aim for variety

There are all sorts of interesting breads and rolls available that are perfect for perking up sandwiches.

- Children love miniature versions of grown-up food; hearty sandwiches can put them off tucking in.
- Look out for mini wholewheat pitas and dinner rolls.
- Flavored wraps are a quick-and-easy way to make sandwiches for large numbers—once filled and rolled they can be sliced into bite-size pieces.
- Sliced bread can be transformed into fun shapes with cookie cutters—try heart- or star-shaped sandwiches for the party princess, farmyard animals, or dinosaurs, and even cars. Use the same shaped cutter to cut out slices of cheese or ham for a neat fit.
- Arrange alternate sandwich squares made with white and wholewheat bread to make a checkerboard display.

Save time

- Chilling a whole loaf of bread will make it easier to cut.
- Don't forget to soften the butter to make it easier to spread.
- Fillings can be made a day ahead, covered, and stored in the refrigerator until you are ready to assemble the sandwiches.
- Rolls and sandwiches can be made up to 3 hours ahead. Cover with a slightly damp dish towel, then tin foil or plastic wrap, and store in the refrigerator.
- Prepare a few plain buttered rolls for fussy eaters.

Quick-and-easy fillings

Each of the following recipes will make enough filling for three sandwiches made with sliced bread.

Egg salad

Put 3 eggs in a small pan and cover with water. Bring to a boil and cook for 6 minutes. Drain and run them under cold water. Shell, then mash the eggs with 2 tbsp. mayonnaise. Stir in mustard to taste.

Tuna and sweet corn

Mix together 1 cup drained canned tuna in spring water with 1½ cups drained canned corn kernels, and 2 tbsp. mayonnaise.

Chunky hummus

Mix together 1½ cups hummus with ¼ chopped cucumber and 4 seeded and chopped tomatoes.

Two-cheese and scallion

Grate 3½oz. (100g) mild cheddar cheese and 3½oz. (100g) Gruyère into a bowl. Stir in 4 finely chopped scallions and 1 tbsp. mayonnaise.

Quick-and-easy dips

Arrange a variety of dips with a pile of tempting, colorful vegetables, such as carrot, celery, and cucumber sticks, slices of colored bell pepper, and cherry tomatoes.

Cherry tomato and pesto

Roughly chop 6 cherry tomatoes and stir into a container of fresh pesto with 2 tbsp. plain yogurt.

Cucumber and yogurt

Seed and chop ¼ cucumber and put into a bowl with 1 tbsp. freshly chopped mint. Stir in ⅔ cup Greek-style yogurt.

Herby cheese

Beat together 1¼ cups herbed cream cheese with 4 tbsp. mayonnaise and 2 tbsp. freshly chopped parsley.

Deluxe Carrot Cake

Prep time: 30 minutes
Cooking time: about 1¾ hours, plus cooling

1 cup sunflower oil, plus extra
to grease
1 cup packed light brown sugar
4 eggs
1¾ cups plus 2 tbsp. all-purpose flour
1 tsp. baking soda
1½ tsp. each apple pie spice and
ground cinnamon
1 orange
1 cup golden raisins
2 cups peeled and coarsely grated
carrots
½ cup chopped walnuts
4 tbsp. drained and chopped
preserved ginger

For the frosting and decoration
2½ cups cream cheese
2 cups confectioners' sugar, sifted
finely grated zest of 1 orange
marzipan carrots (see opposite)

1 Heat the oven to 325°F (300°F for convection ovens). Grease the bottom and sides of an 8in. (20cm) cake pan and line the bottom with parchment paper.

2 Whisk the oil, sugar, and eggs in a large bowl until smooth. Stir in the flour, baking soda, and spices. Finely grate the zest of the orange and add to the mixture with the juice from only half the orange. Add the raisins, carrots, walnuts, and ginger and mix well. Spoon the batter into the prepared pan.

3 Bake for 30 minutes, then cover the top of the cake loosely with foil and bake for 1¼ hours longer, or until a skewer inserted into the middle comes out clean. Let cool in the pan for 5 minutes, then turn out onto a wire rack (leave the lining paper on) and let cool completely.

4 When the cake is cold, peel off the lining paper and cut the cake in two layers horizontally.

Cuts into 12 slices

5 To make the frosting, mix the cream cheese, confectioners' sugar, and orange zest in a bowl. Use half the frosting to sandwich the two cake halves together. Spread the remaining frosting over the top and decorate with marzipan carrots.

To make marzipan carrots

Color 3oz. (75g) marzipan with orange food coloring and ½oz. (15g) with green food coloring. Divide the orange marzipan into 12 pieces and shape them into cones. Mark on ridges with a cocktail pick. Split the green marzipan into 12, then shape into leaf-like fronds and stick to the carrot tops.

The Golden Rules

Cake recipes vary greatly, not only by the methods used to make the cakes, but also in the balance of the various ingredients. There are not any secrets to making a great cake—all you need to do is follow these simple, golden rules.

- If making larger cakes, check first that your oven is big enough. There should be at least 2in. (5cm) oven space all around the cake pan to make sure it bakes evenly.
- Always make sure you have the correct pan shape and size specified in the recipe you are making. The pan sizes required in this book refer to the bottom measurement of the pan.
- Make sure the pan is properly prepared and lined for the recipe you have chosen to make.
- Check that you have all the necessary ingredients stated in the recipe and that they are at the correct temperature.
- Measure and/or weigh out all the ingredients accurately using a measuring cup, measuring spoons, and possibly scales.

- Use the egg sizes stated in the recipe. Substituting different sizes can affect the balance of the cake batter.
- Sifting dry ingredients together helps not only to aerate, but also to disperse lumps.
- Store flours and rising agents in well-sealed packages or airtight containers in a cool, dry place.
- When making cakes by hand, beat well with a wooden spoon until the batter is light and fluffy. This is only possible if your butter is at the correct temperature before you start.
- Be careful not to overprocess or overbeat the batter; the mixture can rise too much in the oven while baking, then collapse and dip in the middle.
- If ingredients have to be folded into a cake batter, use a large

metal spoon, which will cut cleanly through the mixture. Keep scooping down to the bottom of the bowl, then turning the mixture on top of itself, while at the same time giving the bowl a quarter turn. Continue just up until the ingredients are combined—do not be tempted to overfold the cake batter. Try not to be heavy-handed when folding in flour.

- Don't let a cake batter sit around once you've made it: pop it straight into the cake pan and then into the oven, otherwise the rising agents will start to react.
- Before any baking, check the temperature of your oven is correct by investing in an inexpensive oven thermometer.
- Check your oven is heated to the correct temperature stated in the recipe. Once the cake is in the oven, resist the temptation to open the oven door before at least three-quarters of the specified baking time has passed—if you do, the heat will escape and the cake will sink.
- If your cake appears to be browning too quickly, cover the top loosely with tin foil or parchment paper toward the end of the baking time.
- If conditions are cold, the batter will take longer to bake. Similarly, if it is a very hot day, then baking will be slightly quicker.
- Always check the cake is baked 5–10 minutes before the specified baking time, just in case the oven is a little fast.
- After the cake has come out of the oven, let it cool in the pan for the specified time, then turn it out onto a wire rack to cool completely.
- Let the pans cool completely before washing them in warm, soapy water with a nonabrasive sponge.

Genoese Sponge Cake

Prep time: 25 minutes
Cooking time: about 30 minutes or about 40 minutes, plus cooling

3 tbsp. unsalted butter, plus extra
   to grease
½ cup all-purpose flour, plus extra
   to dust
3 extra-large eggs
5 tbsp. superfine sugar
1 tbsp. cornstarch

For the filling and topping

3–4 tbsp. strawberry, raspberry, or
   apricot preserves
½ cup whipping cream, whipped
   (optional)
confectioners' sugar or superfine sugar

1 Grease two 7in. (17.5cm) round cake pans or one deep 7in. (17.5cm) cake pan, then line the bottom(s) with parchment paper and dust the sides with a little flour.

2 Put the butter into a small pan and heat slowly to melt, then take off the heat and let stand for a few minutes to cool slightly.

3 Put the eggs and sugar into a bowl and, using a hand-held electric mixer, beat until blended. Place the bowl over a pan of hot water, making sure the bottom of the bowl doesn't touch the water, and whisk until the mixture is pale and creamy and thick enough to leave a trail on the surface when the whisk is lifted— about 5 minutes. Remove the bowl from the pan and whisk until cool.

4 Heat the oven to 350°F (300°F for convection ovens). Sift the flour and cornstarch into the egg bowl, then use a large metal spoon to carefully fold in, trying to knock out as little air as possible.

5 Pour the melted and cooled butter around the edges of the batter, leaving any butter sediment behind in the pan. Very lightly fold in the butter until it has been incorporated into the batter. Pour into the prepared pan(s).

6 Bake the cake(s) on the middle shelf of the oven for 25–30 minutes for the

cake pans, or 35–40 minutes for the deep pan, until well risen and springy to the touch when lightly pressed in the middle. Loosen the edges with a metal spatula and cool in the pan(s) for 10 minutes. Turn out onto a wire rack (leave the lining paper on) and leave to cool completely.

7 When the cake(s) is cool, peel off the lining paper. Halve the single cake horizontally. Sandwich the two cake layers together with preserves and whipped cream, if you like. Dust with confectioners' sugar, or sprinkle the top with superfine sugar. Serve in slices.

Cappuccino and Walnut Cake

Prep time: 30 minutes
Cooking time: about 35 minutes, plus cooling

4 tbsp. unsalted butter, melted and
 cooled, plus extra to grease
¾ cup plus 1 tbsp. all-purpose flour
1 tsp. baking powder
4 eggs
heaped 1 cup superfine sugar
1 tbsp. chicory and coffee extract
¾ cup toasted, cooled, and finely
 chopped walnuts

For the decoration

½ cups walnuts
1 tbsp. granulated sugar
¼ tsp. ground cinnamon

For the frosting

7oz. (200g) white chocolate, chopped
4 tsp. chicory and coffee extract
2 cups mascarpone

1 Heat the oven to 375°F (325°F for
 convection ovens). Grease two
 8 × 1½in. (20 × 4cm) round cake
 pans and line each with a circle of
 greased parchment paper.

2 Sift the flour and baking powder
 together twice.

3 Using a hand-held electric mixer,
 beat the eggs and superfine sugar in
 a large heatproof bowl set over
 a pan of barely simmering water for
 3–4 minutes until light, thick, and
 fluffy. Take the bowl off the heat and
 continue mixing until the mixture
 has cooled and the mixer leaves
 a ribbon trail for 8 seconds when
 lifted out of the bowl.

4 Fold in the butter, coffee essence,
 and chopped walnuts. Sift half the
 flour into the mixture and, using a
 metal spoon, fold it in carefully, but
 quickly. Sift and fold in the rest of
 the flour, taking care to knock out
 as little air as possible. Divide the
 batter evenly between the prepared

pans and tap them lightly on the work surface.

5 Bake for 20–25 minutes until the cakes spring back when lightly pressed in the middle. Cool in the pans for 10 minutes, then turn out onto a wire rack (leave the lining paper on) and let cool completely. When the cakes are cool, peel off the lining paper.

6 To make the decoration, blend the walnuts with the granulated sugar and cinnamon in a food processor or blender until finely chopped. Take care not to overprocess the nuts or they'll become oily. Set aside.

7 To make the frosting, melt the chocolate slowly without stirring in a heatproof bowl set over a pan of simmering water, making sure the bottom of the bowl doesn't touch the water. In another bowl, add the coffee essence to the mascarpone and beat until smooth, then slowly beat in the chocolate.

Cuts into 10 slices

8 Spread one-third of the frosting on top of one cake, then sandwich with the other cake. Smooth the remaining frosting over the top and side. Lift the cake onto a large piece of parchment paper and scatter the chopped nuts all around it, then lift the parchment up to press the nuts onto the side. Transfer to a plate. Serve in slices.

Test It, Store It

Ovens vary and the time given in the recipe might be too short or too long to correctly bake any cake or other baked goods. Therefore, always test to be confident of a successful result.

Testing sponge cakes

1 Gently press the middle of the sponge cake . It should feel springy (see image, right). If it's a whisked cake, it should be just shrinking away from the side of the pan.

2 If you have to put the cake back into the oven, close the door gently so that the vibrations don't cause the cake to sink in the middle.

Testing fruitcakes

1 To test if a fruitcake is baked, insert a skewer into the middle of the cake (see image, left) and leave for a few moments, then pull it out. If it comes away clean, the cake is ready.

2 If any cake batter sticks to the skewer, the cake is not quite baked, so put it back in the oven for a few more minutes, then test again with a clean skewer.

Cooling cakes

Always follow the cooling instructions specified in the recipe. If certain cakes are left for too long in the pan, they will sweat. Most rich fruitcakes, on the other hand, should be left to cool completely in the pan to help them stabilize. Make sure all cakes are completely cool before frosting or storing.

Storing cakes

With the exception of rich fruitcakes and gingerbread, most cakes are best enjoyed freshly baked. If storage is necessary, however, use a cake tin or large plastic container. Make sure that the cake is completely cool before you put it into the container. Or, wrap the cake in a double layer of parchment paper and over-wrap with tin foil. Avoid putting rich fruitcakes in direct contact with foil—the fruit can react with it. Never store a cake in the same container as cookies, because the cookies will quickly soften.

Most cakes, particularly sponges, freeze well, but they are generally best frozen before filling and decorating. If freezing a finished cake, leave uncovered in the freezer first, then store in an airtight container.

Banana Cake

Prep time: 20 minutes
Cooking time: about 1 hour, plus cooling

1 stick unsalted butter, softened, plus
   extra to grease
½ cup packed light brown sugar
2 extra-large eggs, lightly beaten
scant ¼ cup smooth applesauce
3 very ripe bananas, mashed
1½ tsp. apple pie spice
1 cup plus 3 tbsp. gluten-free
   flour blend
1 tsp. gluten-free baking powder
a pinch of salt

For the frosting

6 tbsp. unsalted butter, softened
1 cup confectioners' sugar, sifted
¼ cup packed light brown sugar
½ tbsp. milk (optional)
dried banana slices to decorate
   (optional)

1 Heat the oven to 350°F (300°F for convection ovens). Grease the bottom and sides of a 9 x 5in. (22.5 x 12.5cm) loaf pan and line with parchment paper.

2 Using a hand-held electric mixer, beat the butter and sugar in a large bowl until pale and creamy. Gradually whisk in the eggs, then the applesauce. Stir in the bananas.

3 Sift the spice, flour, baking powder, and salt into the bowl, then use a large metal spoon to fold in. (The batter might look a little curdled.) Spoon the batter into the prepared pan.

4 Bake for 50 minutes to 1 hour until risen and a skewer inserted into the middle comes out clean. Let cool in the pan for 10 minutes, then turn out onto a wire rack (leave the lining paper on) and let cool completely. When cool, remove the lining paper and put the cake on a serving plate.

5 To make the frosting, whisk together the butter and both sugars until smooth. If needed, add a little milk to loosen. Spread over the top of the cooled cake. Decorate with banana chips, if you like. Serve in slices.

Sticky Gingerbread

Prep time: 20 minutes
Cooking time: 1 hour 15 minutes, plus cooling

1 stick unsalted butter, plus extra
   to grease
heaped ½ cup packed light
   brown sugar
¼ cup molasses
⅔ cup Lyle's Golden Syrup
1 cup all-purpose flour
2 tsp. apple pie spice
5 tbsp. finely chopped preserved
   ginger
2 extra-large eggs
7 tbsp. milk
1 tsp. baking soda
extra molasses or Lyle's Golden Syrup
   to glaze (optional)

1 Put the butter, sugar, molasses, and golden syrup in a saucepan and heat slowly until the butter has melted. Let cool for 5 minutes. Grease and line the bread-maker bowl with parchment paper, if specified in the manual.

2 Sift the flour and apple pie spice together into a bowl. Add the syrup mixture, chopped ginger, eggs, and milk and stir well until combined.

3 In a cup, mix the baking soda with 2 tbsp. hot water, then add to the bowl. Stir the mixture well and pour into the bread-maker bowl.

4 Fit the bowl into the bread maker and follow the manufacturer's directions. Select 1 hour 10 minutes on the timer and choose a light crust. Press start.

5 To check the cake is baked, pierce the middle with a skewer; it should come out fairly clean. If necessary, re-set the timer for a little longer.

6 Remove the bowl from the machine and leave the cake in it for 5 minutes, then turn out onto a wire rack. Brush the top of the cake with the treacle or syrup to glaze, if you like, and let cool.

Lemon Drizzle Loaf

Prep time: 20 minutes
Cooking time: about 50 minutes, plus cooling

1½ sticks unsalted butter, softened, plus extra to grease
¾ cup superfine sugar
4 eggs, lightly beaten
3 lemons
1 cup self-rising flour, sifted
½ cup almond meal
3oz. (75g) sugar cubes

1 Heat the oven to 350°F (300°F for convection ovens). Grease a 9 x 5in. (22.5 x 12.5cm) loaf pan and line with parchment paper.

2 Put the butter and superfine sugar into a large bowl and, using a hand-held electric mixer, cream together until pale and fluffy—this should take about 5 minutes. Gradually beat in the eggs, followed by the finely grated zest of 2 of the lemons and the juice of ½ lemon. Fold the flour and almond meal into the butter mixture, then spoon into the prepared pan.

3 Bake for 40–50 minutes until a skewer inserted into the middle comes out clean. Let cool in the pan for 10 minutes, then turn out, peel off the lining paper, and let cool on a wire rack until just warm.

4 Meanwhile, put the sugar cubes into a small bowl with the juice of 1½ lemons and the pared zest of 1 lemon. (You should have 1 unjuiced lemon left over.) Soak for 5 minutes, then use the back of a spoon to roughly crush the cubes. Spoon over the warm cake and let cool completely before serving in slices.

SAVE TIME

Store in an airtight container. This cake will keep for up to four days.

Fruity Teacake

🍴 **Prep time:** 20 minutes, plus soaking
Cooking time: 1 hour, plus cooling

⅔ cup (150ml) hot black tea, made
   with 2 Earl Grey tea bags
1⅓ cups golden raisins
½ cup roughly chopped ready-to-eat
   dried figs
½ cup roughly chopped prunes
a little vegetable oil
½ cup packed dark brown sugar
2 eggs, beaten
1¾ cups plus 2 tbsp. gluten-free flour
2 tsp. wheat-free baking powder
2 tsp. apple pie spice
butter to serve (optional)

1 Pour the tea into a bowl and add all the dried fruit. Let soak for 30 minutes.

2 Heat the oven to 375°F (325°F for convection ovens). Grease a 9 x 5in. (22.5 x 12.5cm) loaf pan and line with parchment paper.

3 Beat the sugar and eggs together in a large bowl until pale and slightly thickened. Add the flour, baking powder, apple pie spice, and soaked dried fruit and tea, then mix together well. Spoon the batter into the prepared pan and level the surface.

4 Bake on the middle shelf of the oven for 45 minutes to 1 hour. Cool completely in the pan. When the cake is cool, turn out and peel off the lining paper. Serve sliced, with a little butter if you like.

SAVE TIME

Wrap in plastic wrap and store in an airtight container. This cake will keep for up to five days.

Cuts into 12 slices

Cake Troubleshooting

Use this handy guide to help you find out where and why things might have gone wrong with your cake baking.

The cake sinks in the middle
- The oven door was opened too soon.
- The cake was underbaked.
- The ingredients haven't been measured accurately.
- The wrong size cake pan might have been used.

The cake has a cracked, domed top
- The oven temperature was too hot.
- The cake was too near the top of the oven.
- Insufficient liquid was used.
- The baking pan was too small.
- Too much raising agent was used.

The cake has a dense texture
- The batter curdled when the eggs were being added.
- Too much liquid was used.
- The mixture was overfolded.
- Too little rising agent was used or an ineffective rising agent that was too old was used.

The fruit has sunk to the bottom
- The batter was too soft to support the weight of the fruit. This is liable to happen if the fruit was too sticky or wet.

The cake edges are crunchy
- The baking pan was overgreased.

Battenberg Delight

Prep time: 35 minutes
Cooking time: about 35 minutes, plus cooling

1½ sticks unsalted butter, softened, plus extra to grease

¾ cup plus 2 tbsp. superfine sugar

3 extra-large eggs, lightly beaten

1⅔ cups self-rising flour

¼ cup almond meal

a few drops of almond extract

pink and yellow food coloring

3–4 tbsp. lemon curd

confectioners' sugar to dust

1lb. 2oz. (500g) marzipan

1 Heat the oven to 350°F (300°F for convection ovens). Grease a 8in. (20cm) square, straight-sided roasting or brownie pan. Cut a rectangle of parchment paper that measures exactly 8 × 12in. (20 × 30cm). Fold it in half (short end to short end), then make a fold 2in. (5cm) wide down the length of the closed side, bending it both ways to mark a pleat. Open up the parchment, then pinch the pleat back together, so it stands perpendicular to the rest of the parchment. Position the parchment in the bottom of the pan—it should line the bottom exactly and form a 2in. (5cm) divider down the middle.

2 Using a hand-held electric mixer, cream the butter and superfine sugar together in a large bowl until pale and fluffy. Gradually beat in the eggs, then use a large metal spoon to fold in the flour, almond meal, and almond extract.

3 Spoon half the batter into a separate bowl. Use the food coloring to tint one half yellow and the other pink. Spoon one batter into each side of the prepared pan, making sure the parchment doesn't shift, then level the surface.

4 Bake for 30–35 minutes until a skewer inserted into the middle of each side comes out clean. Let cool in the pan.

5 When the cake is cool, turn out of the pan and peel off the lining

paper. Using a bread knife, level the top of each cake and remove any browned edge. Stack the cakes and trim the sides and ends to reveal colored cake. With the cakes still stacked, halve the cakes lengthwise to make four equal strips of cake.

6 Spread a thin layer of lemon curd along one long side of a yellow strip, then stick it to a long side of a pink strip. Repeat with the remaining two strips. Stick the pairs of sponges on top of one another with more curd to give a checkerboard effect, then trim to neaten. Spread the ends of the cake with more curd.

7 Lightly dust the work surface with confectioners' sugar, then roll out one-eighth of the marzipan until ¼in. (0.5cm) thick. Stick to one end of the cake and trim with scissors. Repeat with the other end.

8 Roll out the remaining marzipan into a long strip, ¼in. (0.5cm) thick—it needs to be at least 8½in.

Serves 10

(21cm) wide and 14in (35cm) long. Brush with lemon curd. Place the cake on the marzipan at one of the short ends, then trim the width of the marzipan strip to match the cake. Roll the cake, sticking it to the marzipan as you go. Trim the end to neaten. Serve in slices.

Oven Scones

Prep time: 15 minutes
Cooking time: 10 minutes, plus cooling

3 tbsp. unsalted butter, diced, plus extra to grease

1¾ cups plus 2 tbsp. self-rising flour, plus extra to dust

a pinch of salt

1 tsp. baking powder

about ⅔ cup (150ml) milk

beaten egg or milk to glaze

whipped cream, or butter and preserves to serve

1 Heat the oven to 425°F (400°F for convection ovens). Grease a baking sheet.

2 Sift the flour, salt, and baking powder into a bowl. Cut in the butter until the mixture resembles fine bread crumbs. Using a knife to stir it in, add enough milk to give a fairly soft dough.

3 Gently roll or pat out the dough on a lightly floured work surface to a ¾in. (2cm) thickness and then, using a 2½in. (6.25cm) plain cutter, cut out circles. Put on the prepared baking sheet and brush the tops with beaten egg or milk.

4 Bake for about 10 minutes until golden brown and well risen. Transfer to a wire rack and let cool.

5 Serve warm, split, and filled with whipped cream, or spread with butter and preserves.

TRY THIS

To guarantee a good rise, avoid heavy handling and make sure the rolled-out dough is at least ¾in. (2cm) thick.

Perfect Coffee and Tea

Use this handy guide to help you find out how
much coffee and tea to serve at your event.

Coffee and tea

Ground coffee:	4oz. (125g) for 12 medium cups
Instant:	3oz. (75g) for 12 large cups
Milk:	allow 2 cups (480ml) for 12 cups of tea

Approximate Coffee and Tea Quantities

COFFEE GROUND

24–26 servings:

generous 1 cup coffee
scant 4 quarts (3.4 liters) water
1¾ quarts (1.7 liters) milk
2¼ cups sugar

Notes: If you make the coffee
in advance, strain it after infusion.
Reheat without boiling.

Tea

INDIAN

24–26 servings:

4 tbsp. loose tea
4½ quarts (4.5 liters) water
3¾ cups (900ml) milk
2¼ cups sugar

Notes: It is better to make tea in several
pots rather than in one outsized one.

CHINA

24–26 servings:

4 tbsp. loose tea
5¼ quarts (5 liters) water
2–3 lemons
2¼ cups sugar

Notes: Infuse China tea for 2–3 minutes
only. Put a thin lemon slice in each cup
before pouring. Serve sugar separately.

Irish or Gaelic Coffee

To serve one, you will need:

2 tbsp. Irish whiskey

1 tsp. brown sugar

about ½ cup (125ml) hot double-strength black coffee

1–2 tbsp. heavy cream, chilled

1 Gently warm a glass, pour in the whiskey, and add the sugar.
2 Pour in black coffee to within 1in. (2.5cm) of the brim and stir to dissolve the sugar.
3 Fill to the brim with the chilled cream, poured over the back of a spoon, then let stand for a few minutes.

Liqueur Coffee Around the World

The following are made in the style of Irish Coffee. Allow 2 tbsp. of the liqueur or spirit to ½ cup (125ml) of double-strength black coffee, with sugar to taste—usually about 1 tsp.—and some thick heavy cream to pour on top; these quantities will make 1 glassful:

- ❑ Cointreau Coffee
  (made with Cointreau)
- ❑ Caribbean Coffee
  (made with rum)
- ❑ German Coffee
  (made with kirsch)
- ❑ Normandy Coffee
  (made with Calvados)
- ❑ Russian Coffee
  (made with vodka)
- ❑ Calypso Coffee
  (made with Tia Maria)
- ❑ Witch's Coffee
  (made with strega; sprinkle a little grated lemon zest on top)
- ❑ Curaçao Coffee
  (made with curaçao; stir with a stick of cinnamon)

Garden Party

Stress-Free Get-ahead Time Plan

All these recipes are designed to take the stress out of cooking. Follow this triple-tested time plan using our get-ahead instructions—there'll be no last-minute dashing around when all your guests arrive, and you can be confident that all the food will be a success!

Up to two days ahead

- Make the Salmon Sandwich Stacks
- Make Triumphant Strawberry and Cream Mold

Up to a day ahead

- Make the Coronation Chicken (but don't add the cilantro)
- Make the Layered Omelet Cake
- Make the Cheese and Pickle Crown Bread
- Prepare the Perfect Victoria Sponge Cake
- Prepare Individual Queen of Trifles

On the day

6 hours before your serve

- Prepare Individual Sausage and Egg Pies and cook now—or closer to serving time if you want to eat them warm

4 hours before you serve

- Make the Marmite Cheese Straws

2 hours before you serve

- Prepare the Light and Fresh Potato Salad
- Slice and then chill the Salmon Sandwich Stacks

30 minutes before you serve

- Complete Coronation Chicken
- Add the cress to the Light and Fresh Potato Salad
- Finish off The Perfect Victoria Sponge Cake and Individual Queen of Trifles

When your guests arrive

- Pass the snacks around
- Serve the main courses when you're ready!
- Remember to unmold the gelatin dessert before you start to serve the desserts.

Salmon Sandwich Stacks

Prep time: 10 minutes, plus chilling

2 cups (500g) mascarpone

1 tbsp. roughly chopped capers

finely grated zest and juice of 1 lemon

2 tbsp. freshly chopped dill

1 tbsp. milk

12 medium-thick slices white bread

12oz. (350g) smoked salmon slices

SAVE TIME

Stack, wrap, and chill the sandwiches up to two days ahead. Slice the stacks into rectangles up to 2 hours ahead and keep chilled. Serve when ready.

1 Put the mascarpone, capers, lemon zest and juice, dill, and milk into a large bowl and mix well. Lay the bread on a cutting board and divide half the mascarpone mixture among the slices. Spread evenly to the edges of the bread.

2 Next, divide half the smoked salmon slices over the mascarpone, making sure the fish is in an even layer. (Use scissors to trim if necessary.) Lay another piece of bread on top of each stack, then repeat the process with the remaining mascarpone mixture, smoked salmon, and bread. Wrap the stacks individually in plastic wrap and chill for at least 5 hours, or ideally overnight.

3 Using a large serrated knife, cut the crusts off the sandwich stacks, then slice each stack into six rectangles. Secure each stack with a cocktail pick, if you like, and serve.

Makes 24

Coronation Chicken

Prep time: 20 minutes
Cooking time: about 20 minutes, plus cooling

6 boneless, skinless chicken breast halves

2 tsp. mild curry powder

⅔ cup (150g) mayonnaise

½ cup crème fraîche or sour cream

3 tbsp. mango chutney

1 tsp. Worcestershire sauce

2 celery ribs, thinly chopped

½ cup chopped dried ready-to-eat apricots

⅓ cup golden raisins

⅔ cup slivered almonds

a large handful of fresh cilantro, chopped

salt and freshly ground black pepper

1 Put the chicken breasts into a large pot and cover with cold water. Bring to a boil, then reduce the heat and simmer gently for 15 minutes, or until the chicken is cooked through; slice a breast in half to check. Drain and let cool completely.

2 Meanwhile, heat a small skillet and toast the curry powder, stirring, until it smells fragrant—about 30 seconds. Empty into a large bowl and stir in the next seven ingredients, along with plenty of seasoning.

3 Cut or rip the cooled chicken into bite-size pieces and add to the mayonnaise mixture, along with most of the slivered almonds and chopped cilantro. Stir well and check the seasoning.

4 To serve, garnish with the remaining almonds and cilantro.

SAVE TIME

Prepare the chicken to the end of step 3 up to one day ahead, but don't add the cilantro or garnish. Cover with plastic wrap and chill. To serve, stir the chopped cilantro through and complete the recipe.

Serves 12

Marmite Cheese Straws

TAKE 5

🍴 **Prep time:** 10 minutes
🍴 **Cooking time:** about 20 minutes

2 × 13oz. (375g) bought puff pastry dough
(in rectangular sheets), thawed
if frozen

all-purpose flour to dust

1½ tbsp. Marmite

1½ tbsp. milk

¾ cup each finely grated Parmesan and
Gruyère cheese

1 Heat the oven to 400°F (350°F for
convection ovens). Line cookie sheets
with parchment paper.

2 Unroll one puff pastry dough sheet
onto a lightly floured work surface.
Put the Marmite into a small bowl and
gradually mix in the milk. Brush half
the mixture over the dough.

3 Put both cheeses into another small
bowl and stir to combine, then
sprinkle half the cheese mixture over
the dough. Unroll the second sheet of
dough and place on top of the cheese.
Lightly roll a rolling pin over the
dough to stick the sheets together,
rolling the dough a little thinner in
the process. Brush the top with the
remaining Marmite mixture, then
sprinkle the remaining cheese over
the top, pressing the cheese down to
help it stick. Cut the dough lengthwise
into 12 equal long strips, then halve
to make 24 shorter strips.

4 Transfer the strips to the prepared
cookie sheets and bake for
15–20 minutes until golden brown.
Transfer to a wire rack. Serve warm or
at room temperature.

SAVE TIME

Make the cheese straws up to
4 hours ahead.

Makes 24

Individual Sausage and Egg Pies

Prep time: 30 minutes
Cooking time: about 40 minutes

7 medium eggs

1lb. (450g) sausage meat

1 tbsp. wholegrain mustard

2 scallions, thinly chopped

1 tsp. Italian seasoning

all-purpose flour to dust

2¼lb. (1kg) bought piecrust dough

salt and freshly ground black pepper

1 Bring a large pot of water to a boil and add six of the eggs. Reduce the heat and simmer for exactly 6 minutes. Lift out of the pan with a slotted spoon and run them under cold water to cool quickly. Put to one side.

2 Put the sausage meat, mustard, scallions, Italian seasoning, and some seasoning into a large bowl and mix well. Put to one side.

3 Heat the oven to 425°F (400°F for convection ovens). Lightly dust a work surface with flour and roll out two-thirds of the dough to ⅛in. (0.3cm) thick. Stamp out twelve 4in. (10cm) circles and press the circles

into 12 holes of a muffin pan, working the dough so that it comes just above the edges of the holes. Put the trimmings to one side.

4 Shell the eggs and halve lengthwise through the yolk, which should not yet be completely set. Put one egg half, cut side down, in the bottom of each dough well. Divide the sausage mixture among the wells, carefully pushing it around the eggs and leveling the surface.

5 Roll out the remaining one-third of the dough and trimmings as before and stamp out 3in. (7.5cm) circles. Beat the remaining egg and use some to brush the edges of the pies and the visible sausage meat. Press on the lids and seal the edges. Use a skewer to pierce a hole in the middle of each lid to let steam escape. If you like, reroll any trimmings and use to decorate the pies. Brush the tops with egg.

6 Cook the pies for 30–35 minutes until deep golden brown. Do not turn

Serves 12

off the oven. Cool for 5 minutes in the pan, then remove from the pan and transfer the pies to a baking sheet.

7 Cook the pies for 5 minutes sheet to crisp up the edges. Cool for 10 minutes, then serve warm or at room temperature.

Layered Omelet Cake

Prep time: 30 minutes, plus chilling
Cooking time: about 25 minutes, plus cooling

16 extra-large eggs

5 tbsp. freshly snipped chives

2 tbsp. vegetable oil

2 cups cream cheese

1 red bell pepper, seeded and
finely diced

½ red chili pepper, seeded and thinly
chopped (see Safety Tip, page 38)

1½ cups chopped watercress, plus extra
to garnish

salt and freshly ground black pepper

1 Beat the eggs in a large bowl with
2 tbsp. of the chives and plenty of
seasoning. Heat ½ tbsp. of the oil in
an 8in (20cm) nonstick skillet and
pour in one-quarter of the egg
mixture. Swirl the pan so the bottom
is covered. Using a metal spatula,
occasionally push the mixture in from
the side of the pan while it's cooking,
but ensure the bottom is always
fully covered with egg. Cook for 2–3
minutes until the underside is golden,
then flip the omelet and cook for 2–3
minutes longer. Transfer the omelet to
a plate and let cool completely.

2 Repeat with the remaining oil and
egg mixture to make three more
omelets. (You might need to whisk the
eggs before making each omelet to
redistribute the chives).

3 While the omelets are cooling, beat
together the cream cheese, remaining
chives, the red pepper, chili pepper,
chopped watercress, and some
seasoning in a large bowl. Line an 8in
(20cm) cake pan with plastic wrap and
place a cooled omelet in the bottom.
Spread one-third of the cream cheese
mixture over the omelet. Repeat the

SAVE TIME

Prepare the omelet cake to
the end of step 3 up to one day
ahead. Chill. Complete the
recipe to serve.

Serves 12

stacking and spreading twice more and then top with the remaining omelet. Cover the pan with plastic wrap and chill in the refrigerator for at least 30 minutes.

4 To serve, lift the omelet cake from the pan and peel off the plastic wrap. Transfer to a serving plate or cake stand, garnish with watercress, and serve in wedges.

Light and Fresh Potato Salad

Prep time: 15 minutes
Cooking time: 25 minutes

3lb. 2oz. (1.5kg) new potatoes, unpeeled, chopped into bite-size pieces

7 tbsp. olive oil

2 tbsp. wholegrain mustard

juice of ½ lemon

1¾ cups thinly sliced radishes

4 scallions, thinly sliced

several handfuls of garden cress or watercress

salt and freshly ground black pepper

1 Cook the potatoes in salted boiling water for 15–20 minutes until just tender but not breaking apart.

2 While the potatoes are cooking, whisk together the oil, mustard, lemon juice, and plenty of seasoning.

3 Drain the potatoes and let steam-dry for 5 minutes, then put them back into the pot. Pour the dressing over and add the radishes and scallions. Fold together, trying not to break up the potatoes.

4 Tip into a serving dish and scatter the garden cress or watercress over the top.

TRY THIS

Prepare the potato salad up to a couple of hours ahead, but do not add the garden cress. Transfer to a serving dish, cover with plastic wrap, and chill. Complete the recipe to serve.

Serves 12

Cheese and Pickle Crown Bread

Prep time: 30 minutes, plus rising
Cooking time: about 30 minutes, plus cooling

2 tbsp. butter

1¼ cups (300ml) milk

2 eggs

3⅔ cups all-purpose flour, plus extra to dust

1 tsp. sugar

2 tsp. instant dry yeast

1 tsp. salt

2/3 cup finely chopped sweet pickle or relish

1½ cups grated sharp cheddar cheese

vegetable oil to grease

SAVE TIME

Make up to a day ahead. Cool completely, then wrap in foil. Unwrap and serve.

1 Heat the butter in a small pan until melted. Stir in the milk and heat slowly for 1 minute until just warm. Beat in one of the eggs.

2 Put the flour, sugar, yeast, and salt into a bowl and stir together. Add the milk mixture and stir quickly to make a soft, but not sticky, dough. Add a little more milk and/or flour as needed. Tip the dough on to a lightly floured work surface and knead for 10 minutes. Form into a ball, cover with a clean dish towel, and let rise for 30 minutes.

3 Roll the dough out to make a 10 × 15in. (25 × 37.5cm) rectangle. Put the pickle and cheese into a small bowl and stir to mix, then spread the mixture over the dough, leaving a ½in. (1cm) border. Roll the dough up from one of the long edges to make a rope shape. Use a bread knife to cut 12 slices. Flour a cookie sheet, then arrange the slices on their sides, with the swirls facing sideways and just touching to make a ring shape on the cookie sheet.

Loosely cover with greased plastic wrap and let rise for 30 minutes.

4 Heat the oven to 400°F (350°F for convection ovens). Beat the remaining egg and use to glaze the rolls. Bake for 25–30 minutes until risen, golden, and the rolls feel firm. Carefully transfer the ring to a wire rack and cool completely before serving.

Perfect Victoria Sponge Cake

Prep time: 30 minutes
Cooking time: about 30 minutes, plus cooling

2 sticks unsalted butter, softened, plus extra to grease

1¾ cups plus 2 tbsp. self-rising flour, plus extra to dust

1 cup plus 2 tbsp. superfine sugar

4 eggs

1 tbsp. milk

6 tbsp. loose strawberry preserves

1 cup heavy cream

confectioners' sugar to dust

1 Heat the oven to 350°F (300°F for convection ovens). Lightly grease two 8in. (20cm) round cake pans and line the bottoms with parchment paper. Dust the side of each pan with flour and tap out the excess.

2 Put the butter and superfine sugar into a large bowl and beat together using a hand-held electric mixer until pale and fluffy—about 3 minutes. Gradually add the eggs, beating well after each addition. If the mixture looks as if it might curdle, mix in a few tablespoons of the flour.

3 Sift in the flour and fold together using a large metal spoon. Next, fold in the milk.

4 Divide the batter equally between the prepared pans and level the surface of each. Bake in the middle of the oven for 25–30 minutes until the cakes are golden and springy to the touch when lightly pressed in the middle. Let the cakes cool in the pans for 5 minutes, then turn out, transfer to a wire rack, and let cool completely.

5 Peel off the lining papers. Spread the preserves over the top of one of the sponge cakes. Next, lightly whip the cream in a medium bowl and dollop over the layer of preserves. Top with the remaining sponge cake, then dust with confectioners' sugar. Serve in slices.

Cuts into 10 slices

Individual Queen of Trifles

Prep time: 30 minutes, plus chilling
Cooking time: about 10 minutes, plus cooling

11oz. (300g) pound cake

2–3 tbsp. cream sherry, to taste,
    or orange juice

5 tbsp. raspberry jam

scant 2½ cups raspberries

4 tbsp. custard powder mix

4 tbsp. sugar

2½ cups (600ml) milk

2 tsp. vanilla extract

1¼ cups (300ml) heavy cream

2 tbsp. confectioners' sugar, sifted

about ½ cup crumbled baked meringue

2 tbsp. chopped shelled unsalted
    pistachios

1 Slice the cake into 10 equal slices and roughly crumble each slice into the bottom of a tumbler or small wine glass. Press down lightly. Divide the sherry or orange juice among the glasses, pouring it over the cake.

2 Heat the jam slowly in a pan until it loosens. Add the fresh raspberries and gently stir to coat the berries in the jam. Divide among the glasses.

3 Next, make the custard. Put the custard powder mix and sugar into a pan and gradually whisk in the milk until smooth. Put the pan over a medium heat and bring to a boil, stirring constantly to prevent lumps, then cook until the custard thickens. Take off the heat and stir in the vanilla. Let cool for 15 minutes.

4 Rewhisk the custard to break it up and divide among the glasses. Chill until needed.

5 To serve, lightly whip the cream and confectioners' sugar until the cream just holds its shape. Divide among the glasses, then scatter the meringue and pistachios on top. Serve.

SAVE TIME

Prepare the trifles to the end of step 4 up to one day ahead. Complete the recipe up to 1 hour ahead.

Serves 10

Triumphant Strawberry and Cream Mold

Prep time: 20 minutes, plus chilling
Cooking time: about 5 minutes, plus cooling

11oz. (275g) strawberry jelly cubes

1 tsp. edible gold glitter (optional)

vegetable oil to grease (optional)

½ cup sugar

1 vanilla bean, split lengthwise

1¼ cups (300ml) heavy cream

2½ cups (600ml) milk

8 unflavored gelatin sheets

1 Snip the jelly cubes into pieces and put into a heatproof pitcher. Pour in 1¼ cups (300ml) boiling water and let dissolve, stirring occasionally. Top up with cold water to make 5 cups (1.2 liters). Stir in the glitter, if you like.

2 Pour the strawberry jelly mixture into a 2¾-quart (2.7 liters) nonstick

SAVE TIME

Make the jelly to the end of step 5 up to two days ahead. Chill. Complete the recipe to serve.

kugelhopf mold or large bowl. (If your bowl or mold is not nonstick, grease lightly with a mild-tasting oil). Chill until completely set—about 3 hours.

3 Meanwhile, put the sugar, vanilla bean, cream, and milk into a pan and heat gently, whisking occasionally to help release the vanilla seeds, until the mixture just begins to boil. Take off the heat and let infuse for 15 minutes.

4 Put the gelatin sheets into a bowl, cover with cold water and let soak for 5 minutes. Lift the soaked gelatin out of the water (discard the water), add to the cream pan, then stir to dissolve. (If the cream mixture is not hot enough to dissolve the gelatin, then reheat gently until the gelatin dissolves.)

5 Lift out the vanilla bean and let the cream mixture cool completely—the strawberry layer needs to be fully set before proceeding.

Serves 10

6 Gently pour the cream mixture over the set jelly and leave in the refrigerator to set completely—about 5 hours.

7 To serve, turn the jelly out onto a serving plate. If it doesn't come out easily, dip the bottom of the mold briefly into a bowl of hot water, taking care no water comes in contact with the jelly. Turn out and serve.

Buffet Food

Perfect Buffet Party

Use this handy guide to help you work out quantities of appetizers, main dishes, vegetables, and dressings for your buffet party.

Starters	Portions	Ingredients	Notes
FISH COCKTAIL	1	2oz. (50g) shelled shrimp or crab or lobster meat, 2 lettuce leaves, about 3 tbsp. sauce	Serve in stemmed glasses, garnished with a shrimp or prawn. Serve with lemon wedges.
	12	1½lb. (700g) fish (as above), 1 large lettuce, 1¾ cups (450ml) sauce	
PÂTÉS allow 3 half slices hot toast per person to serve with the pâté	1	3–4oz. (75–125g)	
	12	2½lb. (1.1kg)	
SMOKED SALMON serve with toast as above or with brown bread	1	1½–2oz. (40–50g)	
	12	1¼lb. (550g)	
	25	2½lb. (1.1kg)	
OTHER SMOKED FISH such as smoked trout or mackerel	1	4oz. (125g)	
	12	2½lb. (1.1kg)	
	25	4½–5½lb. (2–2.5kg)	
SOUPS cream, clear, or iced	1	⅔–¾ cup (150–175ml)	
	12	2⅓ quarts (2.3 liters)	
	25	4½ quarts (4.5 liters)	

	Portions	Ingredients	Notes
Main dishes			
DELICATESSEN MEATS	1	3-4oz. (75-125g)	
ham, tongue, salami	12	2¼lb. (1kg)	
	25	5lb. (2.3kg)	
SALMON	1	4-6oz. (125-175g)	
	12	3-4lb. (1.4-1.8kg)	
ROAST TURKEY	10-15	8-11lb. (3.6-5kg)	
	20-30	15-20lb. (6.8-9kg)	
CHICKEN			
joint	1	5-8oz. (150-225g)	Serve hot or cold.
whole	24-26	three 6lb. (2.7kg) birds	
Salad vegetables and dressings			
CARROTS	12	2lb. (900g), grated	
	25	4lb. (1.8kg), grated	
CELERY	12	2-3 heads	
	25	5 heads	
CUCUMBERS	12	1-1½ cucumbers	
	25	2-3 cucumbers	
LETTUCE	12	2-3 lettuces	Dress at last minute.
	25	5-6 lettuces	
BOILED POTATOES	12	1½lb. (700g)	For potato salads.
	25	3lb. (1.4kg)	
TOMATOES	12	1½lb. (700g)	
	25	3lb. (1.4kg)	
FRENCH DRESSING	12	1¼ cups (300ml)	
	25	1¾-2½ cups (450-600ml)	
MAYONNAISE	12	2½ cups	
	25	4¼ cups	

Perfect Buffet Party

Use this handy guide to help you work out quantities of desserts, savories, bread, crackers, sandwiches, butter, and cheese for your buffet party.

Desserts	Portions	Ingredients	Notes
MERINGUES	40 (small meringue halves)	6 egg whites, 1½ cups superfine sugar, 2½ cups (600ml) whipped cream	Sandwich meringue halves together with the whipped cream not more than 2 hours before serving.
PROFITEROLES	6	1 quantity Profiteroles (page 144), ⅔ cup (150ml) whipped cream, 1 quantity chocolate sauce	Fill the profiteroles with the whipped cream not more than 2 hours before serving.
	12–15	2 quantities Profiteroles (page 144), 1¼ cups (300ml) whipped cream, 2 quantities chocolate sauce	
ICE CREAM (bought or homemade)	12 25–30	2 pints (scant 1 liter) 5 pints (2.4 litres)	Soften in refrigerator 30 minutes before serving.

Savories			
CHEESE STRAWS	48	2 x Cheese Straws (page 30)	
SAUSAGE ROLLS	64	4 x Sausage Rolls (page 56)	

	Portions	Ingredients	Notes
RED PEPPER PESTO CROÛTES	48	2 x Red Pepper & Pesto Croûtes	
COCKTAIL SAUSAGES	32	1lb. (450g)	
QUICHE	6–8	8in. (20cm) quiche	

Bread, Crackers, and Sandwiches

	Portions	Ingredients	Notes
BREAD LOAVES	10–12 slices	1 small loaf, about 14oz. (400g)	
	20–24 slices	1 large loaf, about about 1¾lb. (800g)	
	50 slices	1 long loaf, about 3lb. (1.4kg)	
SLICES OF BREAD	1	1–1½ slices	Cut into triangles when serving with a meal.
FRENCH BREAD	6–8	1 small baguette	
	12–15	1 large baguette	
CRACKERS	1	3 crackers	
	30	60 crackers	

Butter

	Portions	Ingredients	Notes
	1	1–2 tbsp. butter	If bread is served with the meal.
	1	2–3 tbsp. butter	If serving cheese as a course.
spreads 10–12 sandwiches		About 1 stick butter	
spreads 10–12 bread rolls		About 1 stick butter	

Cheese

	Portions	Ingredients	Notes
CHEESE (for biscuits)	1	1–1½oz. (25–40g)	Serve a selection of at least four types.
	25	1½–2lb (700–900g)	
CHEESE (for wine and cheese parties)	1	3oz. (75g)	
	25	4½–5lb (2–2.3kg)	

Fresh and Fruity Barley Salad

Prep time: 15 minutes
Cooking time: about 25 minutes

1¼ cups pearl barley

4oz. (125g) tenderstem broccoli, trimmed

2 peaches

½ cucumber, seeded and diced

a small handful of fresh mint, roughly chopped

a large handful of arugula

1 can (15-oz./425g) can chickpeas, drained and rinsed

2 tbsp. balsamic vinegar

1 tbsp. extra virgin olive oil

salt and freshly ground black pepper

1 Put the pearl barley into a large pot and cover well with water. Add some salt and bring to a boil, then reduce the heat and simmer for about 25 minutes until the barley is just tender. Add the tenderstem broccoli for the final 3 minutes of cooking. Drain and put to one side.

2 Meanwhile, peel and halve the peaches, then discard the pits. Cut each peach half into four wedges, then put the wedges into a large serving bowl. Add the cucumber, mint, arugula, and chickpeas.

3 Add the balsamic vinegar, oil, and some seasoning to the peach bowl, then lightly mix through the drained barley mixture. Check the seasoning and serve.

Serves 4

Classic Coleslaw

🍴 **Prep time:** 15 minutes

¼ each red and white cabbage,
  shredded
1 carrot, grated
½ cup finely chopped fresh
  flat-leaf parsley

For the dressing
1½ tbsp. red wine vinegar
4 tbsp. olive oil
½ tsp. Dijon mustard
salt and freshly ground black pepper

1 To make the dressing, put the
  vinegar into a small bowl. Add
  the oil, mustard, and plenty of
  seasoning. Mix well.
2 Put the cabbage and carrot into
  a large bowl and toss to combine.
  Add the parsley.
3 Stir the dressing again, pour over
  the cabbage mixture, and toss well
  to coat.

TRY THIS

For an easy way to get a brand
new dish, make this into
Thai-Style Coleslaw: replace the
red cabbage with a good handful
of fresh bean sprouts, the parsley
with freshly chopped cilantro, and
add 1 seeded and finely chopped
red chili pepper (see Safety Tip,
page 38). For the dressing, replace
the vinegar with lime juice, the
olive oil with toasted sesame oil,
and the mustard with soy sauce.

Serves 6

Jumbo Salmon Blini

Prep time: 20 minutes
Cooking time: about 10 minutes, plus cooling

1¼ cups (300ml) crème fraîche
  or sour cream
grated zest and juice of ½ lemon, plus
  lemon wedges to serve (optional)
1½ cups less 2 tbsp. all-purpose flour
1 tsp. baking powder
3 extra-large eggs, separated
¾ cup plus 2 tbsp. milk
3 tbsp. snipped chives, plus extra
  to garnish
½ tbsp. olive oil
7oz. (200g) smoked salmon slices
salt and freshly ground black pepper
1 tbsp. lumpfish caviar to garnish
  (optional)

1 Mix the crème fraîche, lemon zest and juice, and seasoning together in a small bowl. Put to one side.

2 Sift the flour, baking powder, and a pinch of salt into a large bowl. Make a well in the middle and add the egg yolks and milk. Gradually whisk the flour into the liquid to make a smooth batter.

3 In a separate bowl, whisk the egg whites until they form stiff peaks. Use a large metal spoon to fold the egg whites into the batter, then add the chives and some pepper.

4 Heat the broiler to medium. Heat the oil in a 10in. (25cm) nonstick skillet. Add the batter and cook over medium-low heat for 3–4 minutes until the bottom is golden. Next, broil for 3 minutes until the top is golden and the blini is cooked through. Leave the blini to cool for 30 minutes.

5 To serve, put the blini onto a serving plate or cake stand and spoon the crème fraîche mixture over. Top with smoked salmon and garnish with extra chives, pepper, and lumpfish caviar, if you like. Serve with lemon wedges, if you like.

Serves 8

Broccoli, Gorgonzola, and Walnut Quiche

Prep time: 15 minutes, plus chilling
Cooking time: about 1 hour

14oz. (400g) piecrust dough, thawed
  if frozen
all-purpose flour to dust
1⅔ cups broccoli florets
¾ cup crumbled Gorgonzola
2 eggs, plus 1 egg yolk
1¼ cups (300ml) heavy cream
¼ cup roughly chopped walnuts
salt and freshly ground black pepper

1 Heat the oven to 400°F (350°F for convection ovens). Roll out the dough on a lightly floured work surface until the thickness of a 50-cent coin, then use to line a 9in. (22.5cm) fluted tart pan, 1in. (2.5cm) deep. Prick the bottom all over and chill for 15 minutes. Line with parchment paper and baking beans, then bake for 20 minutes. Remove the paper and beans and bake for 5 minutes longer. Lower the oven setting to 300°F (250°F for convection ovens).

2 Cook the broccoli in boiling water for 3 minutes, then drain and dry on paper towels. Arrange the broccoli in the tart case and dot with the Gorgonzola. Whisk together the eggs and egg yolk, cream, and seasoning, then pour into the case. Scatter the chopped walnut over the surface.

3 Cook the quiche for 40 minutes, or until the filling is set. Serve warm or at room temperature.

FREEZE AHEAD

To freeze, complete the recipe up to one month in advance. Cool the quiche in the pan, then wrap in plastic wrap and freeze. To use, thaw completely, then serve at room temperature, or gently reheat for 20 minutes in an oven heated to 300°F (250°F for convection ovens).

Serves 6

Bean and Broccoli Phyllo Tart

Prep time: 20 minutes
Cooking time: about 40 minutes

2 eggs

1 cup crème fraîche or sour cream

1 cup soy beans, frozen

heaped 1 cup broccoli cut into
   small florets

½ cup chopped sun-dried tomatoes in
   oil, drained

½ cup crumbled feta

small handful of fresh mint
   leaves, chopped

6 sheets phyllo pastry dough, thawed
   if frozen

sunflower oil to brush

salt and freshly ground black pepper

green salad to serve

SAVE TIME

Make up to a day ahead. Cool in
the pan, cover with foil ,and chill.
Serve cold or reheat (covered) for
15-20 minutes in oven heated to
350°F (300°F for convection ovens).

1 Heat the oven to 350°F (300°F for convection ovens). In a large bowl, beat together the eggs, crème fraîche, and some seasoning. In a separate bowl, combine the soy beans, broccoli, tomatoes, feta, and mint. Add three-quarters of the mixture to the egg.

2 Brush the top of one of the phyllo sheets with oil, then lay it in a 8in. (20cm) round, loose-bottomed cake pan, letting the excess hang over the side. Repeat with remaining sheets, overlapping the sheets slightly each time (without any gaps). Pour in the crème fraîche mixture, then scatter over the remaining vegetable mix.

3 Crumple the overhanging dough down inside the pan, above the level of the filling, then brush the pastry with oil. Put the pan on a baking sheet and cook for 35–40 minutes until the filling is set and the pastry is golden. Serve warm or at room temperature with a green salad.

Serves 8

Perfect Cheese

Probably the best place to buy cheese is from a specialist cheese store if you are lucky enough to have access to one, otherwise many supermarkets have a fresh cheese counter offering a good variety of artisan and factory-made cheeses.

Buying and storing cheese

Try to taste first before you commit to buying a cheese, as artisan cheeses will vary within, as well as across, varieties—some cheeses differ according to the time of year, and certain varieties are seasonal. Once you have made your choice, make sure the cheese is freshly sliced to your requirements. Buy only as much or as little as you think you need— your house heating and refrigeration will dry out the cheese once you get it home.

The best way to store cheese is to wrap it in wax paper, then to put into an unsealed plastic food bag or cheese box. Keep in the refrigerator in the least cold area away from the freezer compartment. If you have a whole, rinded cheese, cover the cut surface with plastic wrap.

To enjoy cheese at its best, you should always remove it from the refrigerator at least 2 hours before serving to bring it to room temperature. Loosen the wrapping and remove it just before serving. Provide at least two knives for cutting, so that there is a separate one for blue cheese.

Buying cheese for vegetarians

Some vegetarians prefer to avoid cheeses that have been produced by the traditional method, because this uses animal-derived rennet; most supermarkets and cheese stores, however, now stock an excellent range of vegetarian cheeses, produced using vegetarian rennet. Always check the label when buying.

Selecting for a cheeseboard

Choosing cheeses for a cheeseboard is a matter of satisfying everyone's taste, so a range of flavors from mild to strong, and a variety of textures, is important. Think about shapes and colors, too. If you are serving four cheeses, choose one hard, one soft, one blue, and one goat cheese.

If you are buying from a specialist cheese store or a supermarket cheese counter, ask to try a piece first so that you know what you are getting and can balance the flavors. It is a question of quality rather than quantity, because a few excellent cheeses are more appealing than five or six with competing flavors.

To accompany your cheeses, choose crisp apples, juicy pears, grapes, or figs. Very mild, soft goat cheeses can be eaten with strawberries; slightly harder ones go well with cherry tomatoes or olives. Salad leaves should be bitter—try some Belgian endive, frisée or arugula. Walnuts and celery are excellent with blue cheese. Oatcakes, wheat wafers, and digestive crackers go well with most cheeses, and if you want to serve bread, make sure it is fresh and crusty. Butter should be unsalted.

As for when you serve cheese, some people like it best as an appetizer and others perfer it at the end of a meal, after dessert. The French custom of moving from main course to cheese course is worth considering. It enables you to savor the cheeses before you are too full to enjoy them, and you can carry on eating with the same wine, if you've served red wine with the main course.

Chicken and Vegetable Terrine

Prep time: 40 minutes, plus chilling
Cooking time: 1 hour 2 minutes, plus cooling

2lb. (900g) chicken joints
1 small slice of white bread,
    crusts removed
2 cups (450ml) heavy cream, chilled
1 small bunch of watercress
4oz. (125g) small young carrots
4oz. (125g) French beans, trimmed
    and stringed
10oz. (275g) peas in the pod, shelled
3oz. (75g) small, even-size
    button mushrooms
7oz. (200g) artichoke hearts, drained
butter to grease
salt and freshly ground black pepper
arugula leaves to garnish (optional)

For the sauce

1¼ cups skinned and quartered ripe
    tomatoes
½ cup (125ml) vegetable oil
4 tbsp. white wine vinegar
5 tbsp. tomato paste

1 Cut all the chicken flesh away from the chicken bones; discard the skin and any fat. Finely grind the chicken and the bread. Chill for 30 minutes. Stir the cream, a little at a time, into the chicken mixture with salt and ground black pepper to taste.

2 Trim the watercress and discard the coarse stems. Stir one-third of the chicken mixture into the watercress. Cover both bowls and chill for 2 hours.

3 Heat the oven to 325°F (275°F for convection ovens). The careful preparation of vegetables is essential to the final presentation. Cut the carrots into neat matchstick pieces, 1 x ⅛in. (2.5cm x 0.3cm). Cut the beans into similar-length pieces. Blanch the carrots, beans, and peas for 2 minutes in separate pans of boiling water. Drain.

4 Trim the mushroom stems level with the caps. Cut the mushrooms across into slices ¼in. (0.5cm) thick.

Dice the artichoke hearts into ¼in. (0.5cm) pieces.

5 Grease a 4¼-cup (1.1 liter) terrine with a lid and bottom-line with a rectangular piece of parchment paper, greasing the top of the paper. Take half the watercress and chicken mixture and spread it evenly over the bottom of the terrine. Arrange the carrots in neat crosswise lines over the top, then spread one-quarter of the chicken mixture carefully over the carrots.

6 Lightly seasoning the vegetables as they are layered, sprinkle the peas over the chicken mixture in the dish and put another thin layer of chicken mixture on top. Next, put the mushrooms in crosswise lines and top with the remaining watercress and chicken mixture. Arrange the artichokes on top, cover with half the remaining chicken mixture, arrange the beans in crosswise lines, and cover with the remaining chicken mixture.

7 Put a double sheet of greased parchment paper on top and cover tightly with the lid. Put the terrine in a roasting pan with water to come halfway up the side. Cook in the oven for 1 hour, or until firm.

8 Cool a little and drain off any juices. Invert the terrine onto a serving plate. Cool, then chill for 1 hour before serving.

9 Meanwhile, to make the sauce, puree the tomatoes in a blender or food processor with the oil, vinegar, tomato paste, and seasoning. Rub through a sieve. Chill lightly before serving, then garnish the terrine with some arugula leaves, if you like.

Serves 8

Raised Pork Pie

Prep time: 45 minutes, plus chilling
Cooking time: about 3½ hours, plus cooling

3 or 4 small veal bones
1 small onion, peeled
1 bay leaf
4 black peppercorns
2lb. (900g) boneless leg or shoulder
   of pork, cubed
¼ tsp. cayenne pepper
¼ tsp. ground ginger
¼ tsp. ground mace
¼ tsp. dried sage
¼ tsp. dried marjoram
1 tbsp. salt
½ tsp. ground black pepper
1¼ cups (300ml) milk and water,
   mixed
⅔ cup lard, diced
3⅔ cups all-purpose flour, plus extra
   to dust
1 egg, beaten
salad to serve

1 Put the bones, onion, bay leaf, and peppercorns in a large pot and cover with water. Simmer for 20 minutes, then boil to reduce the liquid to ⅔ cup (150ml). Strain and cool.

2 Mix the pork with the spices and herbs, 1 tsp. salt, and the pepper.

3 Line the bottom of an 8in. (20cm) springform cake pan with parchment paper. Bring the milk, water, and lard to the boil in a pan, then gradually beat it into the flour and the remaining salt in a bowl. Knead for 3–4 minutes.

4 Roll out two-thirds of the dough on a lightly floured surface and mold it into the pan. Cover and chill for 30 minutes. Keep the remaining dough covered. Heat the oven to 425°F (400°F for convection ovens).

5 Spoon the meat mixture and 4 tbsp. cold stock into the pie shell. Roll out the remaining dough to make a lid and put on top of the meat mixture, sealing the dough edges well. Decorate with dough trimmings and make a hole in the middle. Glaze with the beaten egg.

Serves 8

6 Bake for 30 minutes. Cover loosely with foil, lower the oven setting to 350°F (300°F for convection ovens), and bake for 2½ hours longer. Let cool completely.

7 Warm the remaining jellied stock until liquid, then pour into the middle hole of the pie. Chill and serve with salad.

TRY THIS

If you do not have any bones available to make the stock, use 2 tsp. gelatin to 1¼ cups (300ml) stock.

Strawberry Pavlova with Rosewater Syrup

🍴 **Prep time:** 20 minutes
Cooking time: about 40 minutes, plus cooling

10 egg whites

2¾ cups superfine sugar

1¾ tbsp. cornstarch

2¼lb. (1kg) strawberries, hulled

⅔ cup (150ml) dessert wine, such as
   Muscat de Beaumes de Venise

1 tsp. rose water

2½ cups (600ml) heavy cream

3 tbsp. confectioners' sugar, sifted

1 Heat the oven to 300°F (250°F for convection ovens). Line a large cookie sheet with parchment paper. Use a pencil to draw a 11in. (27.5cm) diameter circle on the parchment, then flip it over so the pencil mark is underneath.

2 Using electric beaters, whisk the egg whites in a large, grease-free bowl until stiff, but not dry. Gradually add 2½ cups superfine sugar, whisking all the time, until the mixture is stiff and glossy. Quickly beat in 1 tbsp. cornstarch.

TRY THIS

Cook the meringue, make the strawberry syrup, and hull the strawberries up to one day ahead. Cool the meringue on the cookie sheet, then cover with plastic wrap and store at room temperature. Cool the syrup, then cover and chill. Keep the hulled strawberries covered in the refrigerator. Whip the cream mixture up to 2 hours ahead, then chill. To serve, bring the syrup, strawberries, and cream to room temperature, then complete the recipe.

3 Spoon the mixture onto the prepared cookie sheet within the marked circle, pushing it into peaks at the edge of the circle. Bake for 40 minutes, or until the meringue is firm to the touch and peels away

Serves 10

from the parchment. Transfer to a rack and leave to cool.

4 Meanwhile, put one-fifth of the strawberries with the wine, remaining superfine sugar, and the rose water into a pan. Heat and simmer gently for 5 minutes. Blend until smooth, then push through a fine sieve, discarding the seeds. Return the mixture to the pan and whisk in the remaining cornstarch.

Heat gently for 3–4 minutes until the syrup thickens, whisking constantly to remove any lumps. Take off the heat and leave to cool.

5 Transfer the cooled meringue to a serving plate. Gently whip the cream with the confectioners' sugar until it just holds its shape. Dollop on top of the meringue, then pile on the remaining strawberries. Drizzle the cooled syrup over and serve.

White Chocolate and Pistachio Profiteroles

Prep time: 30 minutes
Cooking time: about 30 minutes, plus cooling

4 tbsp. butter, cubed, plus extra
   to grease
⅔ cup all-purpose flour
2 eggs, well beaten
scant ½ cup pistachios
3oz. (75g) white chocolate, chopped
scant 2 cups (450ml) heavy cream
3 tbsp. confectioners' sugar

1 Put the butter and ½ cup (125ml) water into a large pan. Slowly heat to melt the butter, then bring to a boil. Take off the heat and quickly whisk in the flour. Carry on whisking until the dough comes away from the side of the pan—about 30 seconds. Cool for 15 minutes.

2 Heat the oven to 400°F (350°F for convection ovens) and lightly grease two baking sheets. Gradually whisk the eggs into the pan containing the cooled dough, beating after each addition. Dollop teaspoonfuls of dough on the baking sheets,

spacing them well apart; you should have about 24. Use a damp finger to smooth the tops, then bake for about 25 minutes until puffed and a deep golden color.

3 Take out of the oven and pierce a hole in the bottom of each profiterole with a metal skewer—this will allow steam to escape. Transfer to a wire rack and leave to cool completely.

4 Meanwhile, put the pistachios into a food processor and blend until finely ground. Put to one side. Melt half the white chocolate in a heatproof bowl set over a pan of simmering water, making sure the bottom of the bowl doesn't touch the water. Leave to cool for about 10 minutes.

5 Put the cream and confectioners' sugar into a large bowl and whip until the mixture holds soft peaks. Whisk in half the ground pistachios and the cooled melted white chocolate. Insert a ¼in. (0.5cm) tip

Serves 8

into a pastry bag. Fill the bag with the cream, then pipe into the cooled profiteroles via the steam hole.

6 Stack the profiteroles on a serving plate. Melt the remaining white chocolate as before, then drizzle over the profiteroles. Scatter the remaining pistachios over them and serve.

TRY THIS

For convenience, complete the recipe to the end of step 5 up to one day in advance, then chill. Complete the recipe up to 3 hours ahead and chill until ready to serve.

Rose Chocolates

Prep time: 10 minutes, plus freezing
Cooking time: about 1 minute

2oz. (50g) white chocolate, chopped

2oz. (50g) milk chocolate, chopped

2oz. (50g) semisweet chocolate, chopped

a selection of sprinkles, colored sugar, gold leaf, and sugar roses to decorate

1 Put each type of chocolate into a small, microwave-safe bowl. Put the bowls side by side in the microwave and heat on full power for 1 minute. Continue heating for 10-second bursts until the chocolates are melted and smooth; you might need to take them out at different times.

2 Meanwhile, line two cookie sheets with parchment paper. Drop scant teaspoonfuls of the different types of melted chocolate onto the prepared sheets, spacing a little apart, then smooth into circles with the back of a teaspoon.

3 Decorate the chocolates with sprinkles, colored sugar, gold leaf, and sugar roses. Put in the freezer for 10 minutes to set, then pack into a tissue-lined box and serve with coffee.

Makes about 36

Drink Me

Wine and Drinks Guide

Use this handy guide to help you work out how much alcohol to factor in for your event.

- For large gatherings, offer one white and one red wine, sticking to around 12.5 percent alcohol, and have plenty of different soft drinks. Provide beer if you like, but avoid hard liquor. Wines, sparkling wines, and hot or cold punches are ideal party drinks.
- For very large numbers, try to buy wines and champagne on a sale-or-return basis. Mineral water, fruit juices, and soft drinks might also be bought in this way.
- Wine boxes can be good value, and it is worth asking your local wine merchant for their advice —some are better than others. If you prefer to serve wine from the bottle, look at the cost-saving potential of buying by the case.
- When it comes to choosing wine it makes sense to find a supplier you can trust, whether it be a supermarket, wine merchant, or discount club. If you opt for something different, just buy one bottle and see if you enjoy it before making spending a significant amount of money.
- Generally, red wine goes best with red meats, and white wine is the better complement to fish, chicken, and light meats, but there really are no longer any hard-and-fast rules.
- For an aperitif, it is nice to serve a glass of chilled champagne or sparkling wine, or a dry sherry.
- Avoid sweet drinks, or liquor with a high alcohol content, as these tend to take the edge off the appetite, rather than stimulating it. Wine or sherry can be served with a soup course. A full-bodied red wine is an excellent accompaniment to the cheeseboard, although some people prefer to drink port wine with their cheese. You might wish to serve a dessert wine, such as Sauternes, or a glass of fruity, semisweet champagne.

Coffee follows, with brandy and liqueurs if you like.

How much to buy?

If you allow one bottle (750ml) of wine per head you should have more than enough. One standard bottle of wine, sparkling wine, or champagne will give six glasses. For a dinner party, allow one or two glasses of wine as an aperitif, one or two glasses with the first course, two glasses with the main course, and another with the dessert or a cheeseboard.

Remember to buy plenty of mineral water—sparkling and still— and fresh fruit juices. For every ten guests, buy two large bottles of sparkling water and a similar amount of still water.

Serving wine

Warm white wine and champagne is inexcusable, and chilled red wine (unless young and intended for serving cold) is not at all pleasant. The ideal temperature for red wine is 59–64°F, with the more tannic wines benefiting from the higher temperature. On a warm day, a brief spell in the refrigerator will help red wine. For whites, the more powerful wines, like Chardonnay, should be served cool rather than cold, at 52–59°F, while other whites should be properly cold, at 43–50°F. Party food will probably take up your available refrigerator space, so you will need plenty of ice to keep drinks cool.

If you have a lot of wine to chill, use the bath, or a large deep sink, if you have one. About an hour before the party, half-fill the bath with ice, pour in some cold water and stand the bottles upright, making sure the ice and water come up to their necks. Alternatively, use a clean plastic garbage pail or cool boxes as containers. (Some hire companies will rent special plastic containers for cooling wines.)

A large block of ice added to chilled water is a good idea. Make this by filling a large strong plastic bag with water, seal securely, and place in the freezer until frozen.

Elderflower Fizz

🍴 **Prep time:** 1 minute

about ¾ cup plus 2 tbsp. apple juice
7 tbsp. elderflower liqueur
chilled sparkling white or rosé wine
apple slices and mint sprigs to garnish

1 Half-fill four champagne flutes with
the apple juice, then add one-quarter
of elderflower liqueur to each glass
and top up with chilled sparkling
wine.
2 Garnish with a slice of apple and
a sprig of mint.

HEALTHY TIP

For a thirst-quenching non-
alcoholic elderflower fizz, just
replace the wine with chilled
sparkling water.

Serves 4

Champagne Cocktail

Prep time: 5 minutes

½ cup (125ml) Grand Marnier

5 tbsp. grenadine

1 large orange, cut into 8 wedges

8 sugar cubes

1 bottle (750ml) champagne, cava, or other sparkling wine, chilled

1 Measure out the Grand Marnier and grenadine and divide among eight champagne glasses. Add an orange wedge and a sugar cube to each glass.

2 Top up the glasses with the champagne, cava, or sparkling wine and serve immediately.

Take 5 Classic Cocktails

Whiskey Sour
To serve one you will need:
juice of ½ lemon, 1 tsp. sugar, 2 tbsp. rye whiskey, and crushed ice.

1 Mix together the lemon juice, sugar, and whiskey, then shake well with the ice.
2 Serve in a whiskey tumbler.

Margarita
To serve one you will need:
2 tbsp. lemon or lime juice, plus extra for dipping, ½ cup (125ml) tequila, 2 tbsp. curaçao, and salt.

1 Dip the edges of a chilled glass into lemon juice and then salt.
2 In a shaker, mix the tequila, curaçao, and lemon or lime juice.
3 Strain into the chilled glass and serve immediately.

Mimosa
To serve one you will need:
juice from 1 small orange and ⅔ cup (150ml) champagne.

1 Strain the orange juice into a champagne flute and top up with chilled champagne. Serve at once.

Piña Colada
To serve one you will need:
5½ tbsp. white rum, ½ cup (125ml) pineapple juice, 4 tbsp. coconut cream, crushed ice, and 1 pineapple slice and 1 cherry to decorate.

1 Blend together the rum, pineapple juice, coconut cream, and the crushed ice.
2 Pour into a large goblet or a hollowed-out pineapple half.
3 Decorate with a slice of pineapple and a cherry. Serve with straws.

Daiquiri

To serve one you will need:
juice of ½ lime or ¼ lemon,
1 tsp. sugar, 2 tbsp. white rum,
crushed ice, and extra fruit juice
and superfine sugar to frost.

1 Mix the fruit juice, sugar, and
   rum in a shaker, add the crushed
   ice, and shake well.
2 Dip the edges of the glass into
   a little more fruit juice and then
   into superfine sugar to frost the
   rim before filling.

Alcoholic drinks and vegetarians

Animal-derived ingredients,
such as gelatin (from cattle) and
isinglass (from fish) are often used
as fining agents in wine, sherry,
port wine, beer, and alcoholic cider.
For this reason some vegetarians
prefer to drink only vegetarian
alternatives. You can find these in
supermarkets and online. Hard
liquor—apart from some malt
whiskies, which have been matured
in sherry casks—and many liqueurs
are generally acceptable
to vegetarians.

Rum Punch

juice of 1 lime
2 tsp. superfine sugar
4 tbsp. dark rum
1 dash Angostura bitters
4–5 ice cubes
soda or mineral water, chilled
lime slices

1 Mix the lime juice and sugar in a tall glass. Add the rum, Angostura bitters, and ice cubes.

2 Top up with soda or mineral water, add some slices of lime and serve immediately.

Serves 4

Cranberry Crush

🍴 **Prep time:** 5 minutes

1 bottle (750ml) sparkling wine, such
  as cava, chilled

1¼ cups (300ml) Calvados

4¼ cups (1 liter) cranberry juice,
  chilled

2 cups (450ml) sparkling water, chilled

1 small orange, thinly sliced

10–12 ice cubes

1 Pour the sparkling wine, Calvados,
  and cranberry juice into a large
  glass bowl.

2 Just before serving, pour in the
  sparkling water and stir, then add
  the orange slices and ice cubes.
  Ladle into glasses and serve
  immediately.

HEALTHY TIP

For an alternative flavor, use
pomegranate juice instead of
cranberry, and add a spoonful of
fresh pomegranate seeds to each
glass instead of orange slices.

Serves 14

Bloody Mary

🍴 **Prep time:** 2 minutes

1 tbsp. Worcestershire sauce
1 dash of Tabasco
2 tbsp. vodka, chilled
⅔ cup (150ml) tomato juice, chilled
ice cubes
lemon juice to taste
celery salt to taste
1 celery rib, with the leaves left on,
  to serve

1 Pour the Worcestershire sauce,
   Tabasco, vodka, and tomato juice
   into a tall glass and stir.
2 Add ice cubes and the lemon juice
   and celery salt to taste. Put the
   celery stick in the glass and serve.

HEALTHY TIP

For a Virgin Mary, just omit
the vodka to transform this
into a non-alcoholic cocktail.

Easy Eggnog

🍴 **Prep time:** 10 minutes

3 eggs
5 tbsp. sugar
4 tbsp. brandy (optional)
7 tbsp. whole milk
freshly grated nutmeg, to garnish

1 Put the eggs into a large bowl. Add the sugar and beat together with a stick blender until thick and moussey—about 5 minutes. Quickly add the brandy, if you like, followed by the milk. Divide among eight small glasses. Garnish with nutmeg and serve.

Serves 8

Mulled Wine

🍴 **Prep time:** 10 minutes, plus infusing
🍴 **Cooking time:** about 15 minutes

2 oranges

6 cloves

1 bottle (750ml) fruity red wine

4 tbsp. brandy or Cointreau

1 cinnamon stick, broken

½ tsp apple pie spices

2 tbsp. sugar

1 Cut one of the oranges into six wedges and push a clove into each wedge. Using a vegetable peeler, carefully pare the zest of the other orange into strips.

2 Put the clove-studded orange wedges in a stainless-steel pan, along with the red wine, brandy or Cointreau, cinnamon stick, apple pie spices, and sugar. Warm slowly over low heat for 10–15 minutes, then remove the pan from the heat and set aside for 10 minutes to let the flavors infuse.

3 Strain the wine into a serving pitcher through a nonmetallic sieve to remove the orange wedges and the cinnamon. Serve in heatproof glasses with a strip of orange zest and a piece of the cinnamon stick draped over each glass.

SAVE TIME

Choose a bold, fruity red—nothing too oaky—such as one from Bordeaux or another wine made from Cabernet Sauvignon or Merlot.

Serves 6

Take 5 Non-alcoholic Drinks

Elderflower Cordial

To make about 4¼ cups (1 liter)
you will need:
10 cups sugar, just over 5 tbsp. citric
acid, 2 sliced lemons, 20 large,
young elderflower heads (shake to
release any insects).

1 Bring 4¼ cups (1 liter) water to
   a boil. Add the sugar and stir
   until dissolved.
2 Add the citric acid and lemon
   slices. Stir in the flower heads.
   Leave overnight, covered.
3 In the morning, strain. If you
   want it clearer, strain again
   through cheesecloth or a coffee
   filter. Bottle, give some away, and
   keep the rest in the refrigerator—
   it will last for months!

Warming Ginger Soda

To serve six, you will need:
11oz. (300g) thinly slice, unpeeled
fresh root, 1 cup superfine sugar, the
grated zest and juice of 1½ lemons,
4¼ cups (1 liter) soda water.

1 Put the fresh ginger into a pan
   with the sugar and lemon zest
   and juice. Add about 2½ cups
   (600ml) cold water to cover. Heat
   slowly to dissolve the sugar, then
   turn up the heat and simmer for
   10 minutes.
2 Strain through a fine sieve
   into a pitcher. Let cool for at least
   10 minutes, then top up with
   soda water.

SAVE TIME

Make syrup up to three days ahead.
Chill. Add soda to serve.

"Still" Lemonade

To make about 4¼ cups (1 liter),
you will need:
3 lemons, ¾ cup plus 2 tbsp. sugar.

1 Remove the lemon zest thinly
   with a potato peeler.
2 Put the zest and sugar into a
   bowl or large, heatproof pitcher
   and pour on 3¾ cups (900ml)
   boiling water over. Cover and let
   cool, stirring occasionally.
3 Add the juice of the lemons
   and strain the lemonade. Serve
   chilled.

Cranberry Cooler

To serve one you will need:
ice cubes, 5 tbsp. cranberry juice,
lemonade or sparkling water,
chilled, 1 lemon slice to serve.

1 Half-fill a tall glass with ice and
   pour in the cranberry juice.
2 Top up with lemonade. If you'd
   prefer the drink to be less sweet,
   double the amount of cranberry
   juice and top up with sparkling
   water. Stir well and serve with
   a slice of lemon.

Fruity Carrot with Ginger

To serve two you will need:
2 oranges, ½in. (1cm) piece of
fresh ginger, peeled and roughly
chopped, ⅔ cup (150ml) freshly
pressed apple juice or 2 eating
apples for juicing, ⅔ cup (150ml)
freshly pressed carrot juice or
3 carrots for juicing, fresh mint
leaves to decorate.

1 Using a sharp knife, cut a slice
   of orange and set aside for the
   decoration. Cut off the peel from
   the oranges, removing as much
   white pith as possible. Roughly
   chop the flesh, discarding any
   seeds, and put into a blender.
   Add the chopped ginger.
2 Pour in the apple and carrot
   juices and blend until smooth.
   Divide between two glasses,
   decorate with quartered orange
   slices and a mint leaf and serve.

398 cal ♥ 18g protein
15g fat (7g sat) ♥ 4g fiber
47g carb ♥ 2.5g salt

8

90 cal ♥ 2g protein
5g fat (1g sat) ♥ 0.5g fiber
10g carb ♥ 0.3g salt

10

90 cal ♥ 4g protein
6g fat (1g sat) ♥ 2g fiber
8g carb ♥ 0.3g salt

16

336 cal ♥ 11g protein
6g fat (1g sat) ♥ 2g fiber
62g carb ♥ 0.7 salt

18

Calorie Gallery

147 cal ♥ 5g protein
13g fat (2g sat) ♥ 2g fiber
3g carb ♥ 0g salt

38

8 cal ♥ 0.1g protein
0g fat ♥ 0.2g fiber
2g carb ♥ 0.1g salt

40

43 cal ♥ 3g protein
2g fat (1g sat) ♥ 0.2g fiber
3g carb ♥ 0.2g salt

42

38 cal ♥ 2g protein
3g fat (1.5g sat) ♥ 0g fiber
0g carb ♥ 0.2g salt

52

42 cal ♥ 1g protein
3g fat (1g sat) ♥ 0.2g fiber
3g carb ♥ 0.2g salt

54

132 cal ♥ 3g protein
9g fat (3g sat) ♥ 0.4g fiber
11g carb ♥ 0.4g salt

56

302 cal ♥ 6g protein
17g fat (10g sat) ♥ 0.3g fiber
34g carb ♥ 0.2g salt

74

582 cal ♥ 9g protein
46g fat (23g sat) ♥ 1g fiber
35g carb ♥ 0.3g salt

76

for 10 slices: 363 cal
3g protein ♥ 18g fat (11g sat)
1g fiber ♥ 50g carb ♥ 0.4g salt

80

341 cal ♥ 4g protein
12g fat (7g sat) ♥ 0.8g fiber
58g carb ♥ 0.7g salt

82

195 cal ♥ 5g protein
1g fat (0.2g sat) ♥ 1g fiber
34g carb ♥ 0.3g salt

20

70 cal ♥ 3g protein
3g fat (1g sat) ♥ 1g fiber
9g carb ♥ 0.3g salt

24

72 cal ♥ 2g protein
2g fat (0.5g sat) ♥ 0.5g fiber
12g carb ♥ 0.3g salt

28

96 cal ♥ 3g protein
6.5g fat (4g sat) ♥ 0.3g fiber
6.3g carb ♥ 0.3g salt

30

140 cal ♥ 6g protein
10g fat (3g sat) ♥ 0.3g fiber
7g carb ♥ 0.6g salt

44

57 cal ♥ 2g protein
3g fat (2g sat) ♥ 0.3g fiber
6g carb ♥ 0.3g salt

46

52 cal ♥ 2g protein
3g fat (1g sat) ♥ 0.5g fiber
6g carb ♥ 0.1g salt

48

36 cal ♥ 1g protein
4g fat (0.5g sat) ♥ 0.1g fiber
1g carb ♥ 0.2g salt

50

105 cal ♥ 2g protein
7g fat (1g sat) ♥ 0.4g fiber
4g carb ♥ 0.3g salt

58

24 cal ♥ 3g protein
1g fat (0g sat) ♥ 0.1g fiber
0g carb ♥ 0.1g salt

60

without cream:
73 cal ♥ 2g protein
0g fat ♥ 0.8g fiber
18g carb ♥ 0g salt

62

without marzipan carrots:
697 cal ♥ 7g protein
48g fat (18g sat) ♥ 1g fiber
62g carb ♥ 0.9g salt

70

for 8 slices: 424 cal
6g protein ♥ 25g fat (13g sat)
1g fiber ♥ 46g carb ♥ 0.3g salt

84

185 cal ♥ 3g protein
1g fat (trace sat) ♥ 2g fiber
42g carb ♥ 0.1g salt

86

555 cal; 7g protein
31g fat (11g sat) ♥ 2g fiber
63g carb ♥ 0.5g salt

90

140 cal ♥ 3g protein
5g fat (3g sat) ♥ 0.9g fiber
22g carb ♥ 0.7g salt

92

140 cal ♥ 6g protein
11g fat (6g sat) ♥ 0.3g fiber
6g carb ♥ 0.8g salt

100

292 cal ♥ 21g protein
19g fat (5g sat) ♥ 0.8g fiber
10g carb ♥ 0.7g salt

102

150 cal ♥ 4g protein
10g fat (7g sat) ♥ 0.2g fiber
11g carb ♥ 0.5g salt

104

per pie: 508 cal ♥ 13g protein
35g fat (28g sat) ♥ 2g fiber
37g carb ♥ 2.0g salt

106

229 cal ♥ 5g protein
6g fat (3g sat) ♥ 1g fiber
43g carb ♥ 0.4g salt

116

294 cal ♥ 5g protein
17g fat (11g sat) ♥ 0g fiber
31g carb ♥ 0.1g salt

118

371 cal ♥ 13g protein
7g fat (1g sat) ♥ 6g fiber
70g carb ♥ 0.5g salt

126

616 cal ♥ 19g protein
54g fat (23g sat) ♥ 4g fiber
8g carb ♥ 0.6g salt

138

617 cal ♥ 31g protein
37g fat (14g sat) ♥ 2g fiber
45g carb ♥ 2g salt

140

614 cal ♥ 5g protein
32g fat (20g sat) ♥ 1g fiber
78g carb ♥ trace salt

142

143 cal ♥ 0g protein
0g fat ♥ 0g fiber
8g carb ♥ 0g salt

158

114 cal ♥ 0g protein
0g fat ♥ 0g fiber
10g carb ♥ 0g salt

160

96 cal ♥ 0.3g protein
0g fat ♥ 0.2g fiber
9g carb ♥ 1.8g salt

162

90 cal ♥ 3g protein
3g fat (1g sat) ♥ 0g fiber
10g carb ♥ 0.1g salt

164

321 cal ♥ 12g protein
31g fat (15g sat) ♥ 0.3g fiber
1g carb ♥ 0.8g salt

108

149 cal ♥ 3g protein
7g fat (1g sat) ♥ 2g fiber
21g carb ♥ 0.3g salt

110

239 cal ♥ 10g protein
8g fat (4g sat) ♥ 1g fiber
34g carb ♥ 1.2g salt

112

527 cal ♥ 5g protein
35g fat (21g sat) ♥ 0.5g fiber
52g carb ♥ 0.3g salt

114

79 cal ♥ 0.5g protein
7g fat (1g sat) ♥ 1g fiber
3g carb ♥ 0.1g salt

128

306 cal ♥ 13g protein
20g fat (11g sat) ♥ 0.7g fiber
19g carb ♥ 1.6g salt

130

683 cal ♥ 12g protein
57g fat (27g sat) ♥ 2g fiber
33g carb ♥ 1g salt

132

298 cal ♥ 7g protein
21g fat (11g sat) ♥ 2g fiber
20g carb ♥ 0.7g salt

134

per profiterole:
496 cal ♥ 5g protein
44g fat (25g sat) ♥ 0.7g fiber
20g carb ♥ 0.3g salt

144

22 cal ♥ 0.3g protein
1.2g fat (0.7g sat) ♥ 0.1g fiber
3g carb ♥ 0g salt

146

112 cal ♥ 0.2g protein
0g fat ♥ 0g fiber
15g carb ♥ 0g salt

152

134 cal ♥ 0g protein
0g fat ♥ 0g fiber
16g carb ♥ 0g salt

154

120 cal ♥ 0g protein
0g fat ♥ 0g fiber
5g carb ♥ 0g salt

166

Index

PICTURE CREDITS
Photographers: Marie-Louise
Avery (pages 29 and 83); Nicki
Dowey (pages 9, 11, 15, 87, 129,
155, 159, 161, 163 and 167);
Will Heap (page 14); William
Lingwood (pages 75 and 78B);
Gareth Morgans (pages 17, 71, 81,
91, 127 and 153); Myles New (25,
26, 39, 41, 43, 47, 51, 53, 55, 57, 63,
101, 103, 105, 107, 109, 111, 113, 115,
117, 119, 133, 135 and 165); Craig
Robertson (pages 27, 32, 33, 78T
and 93); Sam Stowell (pages 45,
49, 59 and 61); Lucinda Symons
(pages 19, 21, 31, 77, 139 and 141);
Philip Webb (page 131);
Kate Whitaker (pages 85, 143,
145, and 147).

Home Economists:
Joanna Farrow, Emma Jane
Frost, Teresa Goldfinch, Alice
Hart, Lucy McKelvie, Kim
Morphew, Aya Nishimura,
Bridget Sargeson, Kate Trend
and Mari Mererid Williams.

Stylists: Tamzin Ferdinando,
Wei Tang, Helen Trent and
Fanny Ward.